ALSO BY MINNA ZALLMAN PROCTOR

Do You Hear What I Hear? Religious Calling,
The Priesthood, and My Father

As Coauthor

I Sang the Unsingable: My Life in Twentieth-Century Music
with Bethany Beardslee

As Translator

These Possible Lives
by Fleur Jaeggy

Belief or Nonbelief? A Confrontation
by Umberto Eco and Carlo Maria Martini

The Angel of History
by Bruno Arpaia

Federico Fellini: His Life and Work
by Tullio Kezich

Love in Vain: Selected Stories
by Federigo Tozzi

In Every Sense Like Love: Stories
by Simona Vinci

What We Don't Know About Children
by Simona Vinci

Landslide

True Stories

| Minna Zallman Proctor |

Catapult   New York

This is a work of nonfiction. However, certain names, identifying characteristics, and locales have been changed to protect the privacy of the people involved.

Published by Catapult
catapult.co

ISBN: 978-1-936787-61-6

Catapult titles are distributed to the trade by Publishers Group West.
Phone: 866-400-5351

Library of Congress Control Number: 2016952070

Printed in the United States of America

9 8 7 6 5 4 3 2 1

for Arlene Zallman
1934–2006

I didn't go to the moon. I went much further—for time is the longest distance between two places.

—Tennessee Williams

Contents

Landslide

Preface: On Faith and Reason

My kids always seem to have their most intense conversations in the backseat of the car. Or maybe that's just when they have conversations that I hear, but I suspect that it is also one of the only times in their day when they are sitting side by side, with nothing to distract them and no one besides each other to answer to. My son, Isaac, might reflect on death as we pass the graveyard between our apartment in Brooklyn and school, or he will talk about how looking at the stars makes him feel awestruck and sick with fear at the same time. The two of them will navigate our complex family structure, who's related to whom and what difference it makes. My daughter, Anna, will say how funny it is that Isaac has a baby brother she's not related to and wonder if Isaac thinks it's funny and he'll say no, it's not funny but that in a way she *is* kind of related to him and yes maybe it is funny after all. They'll review all the grandparents, living and dead, the distinctions between first and second marriages moot by now. From my point of view, they're strolling through a minefield of bad blood, grudges, hurt feelings, and rifts. But they didn't live through all of that and so it doesn't matter. The slightest shift of perspective and it's all obsolete.

"Isaac," Anna said the other day, picking up one of his seven-hundred-page fantasy adventure tomes from the floor of the car, "this is a terrible unicorn." She was referring to the picture on the cover.

"Anna, not all unicorns are good."

"No, this is a bad unicorn. He's scary." The unicorn in the picture had blood on its horn and a fierce look in its eye.

"Unicorns don't have to be all rainbows and glitter, Anna. Some unicorns fight."

"No. Unicorns love people and protect them."

"Some unicorns hurt people. They were just invented as characters and can be all different ways. They can even be monsters. You just think that unicorns are supposed to be all loving and perfect."

"I know what unicorns are supposed to be like." Anna, who was seven, had been waging this battle on many fronts as the children around her had stopped believing in so many of the original tall tales, Santa Claus and the Tooth Fairy (with whom Anna has an avid correspondence).

"Anna, have you ever heard of the Brothers Grimm?" Isaac is two years older than his sister and takes full advantage of his superior knowledge.

"Yes," she lied.

"The Brothers Grimm were two brothers who wrote all these stories, hundreds of years ago. Everything took place in ancient dark forests that had monsters in them. *They* invented unicorns. Anna, you should know this."

"No, they didn't. Unicorns are real and they don't scare people."

"They do and they're invented! There's a unicorn that terrorizes an entire village in one of the stories."

"Isaac, do you know what the problem is? Do you know what the point is? You believe in books, right?"

"Right."

"You believe in books and authors and words on the page."

"Yes. Of course."

"But that's the point, Isaac. You believe in books and I—I believe in unicorns."

Folie à deux

The statement is pointless
The finger is speechless
—R. D. Laing, *Knots*

Instead of kicking me out of tenth grade, or even giving me detention for that matter, Ms. Morand (vice principal of discipline) remanded me to psychological evaluation. Ms. Morand was a stealth intellectual, posing as a former PE specialist, six feet tall with an unforgiving haircut. She was frank with me: if I wasn't going to smoke in the bathroom, threaten other students with a pocket knife, or present convincing evidence of an unsafe home environment, there was no structure built into our school system to address my chronic truancy. It was plain crazy to cut classes four days out of five.

When I met the graduate student assigned to evaluate me in the broom closet off the lobby with a table in it, she seemed out of her league—not least because our appointment was scheduled during remedial geometry, a class I'd only ever been to twice that semester. She gave me a blank piece of paper and told me she was going to ask me some questions and I should write down the answers. "How many questions?" I asked. "Don't worry about that," she answered. Feeling for some reason like Harriet the Spy, I positioned myself in the upper left-hand corner of the paper and waited for a battery of questions.

"You see how your writing is so cramped and small?" I was told four questions later. "It indicates anxiety, fearfulness, and insecurity."

"Or," I countered, "that I didn't know how many questions you were going to ask and how much room I would need."

At our next meeting, the graduate student and I discussed my nightmares. She suggested that I drink warm milk and eat turkey at night before bed. She also recommended that I start keeping a dream journal—unwittingly triggering what would become a chronic lifelong hyper-responsiveness to my REM state, diametrically opposed to the intended purpose of easing my mind. I would go on to spend nights on end struggling to recapture fleeting dream imagery and speculate on its deeper, darker significance.

I was graduated to a professional psychologist, an expert in teenage girls who worked at an elite asylum for teenage girls with eating disorders, which happened to be tucked into a leafy cul-de-sac ten minutes from my house. The grounds seemed aspirational—the institution of choice for future Sylvia Plaths. The doctor's office was beige in every respect and the doctor's features aggressively nondescript, beige, like his walls. "How do you feel about that?" he asked in our first meeting, confusing me. He rephrased, "How does that make you feel?"

I started cutting therapy appointments too. When he finally called to remind me that I had a contract with the school to see him, I complained that our sessions were boring, that he was boring. I hated silence and craved interaction. I told him I thought his beige blinds were better conversationalists than he was and before hanging up, for good measure, I compared him to a turtle.

I'd argue that I'd never really been *in therapy* before I started seeing Doctor Wilk a decade later, a graduate student with a thesis due and a crippling case of writer's block.

NO WONDER I had writer's block. The stories I was trying to write for my thesis were a combination of painful and painfully horrible. There was one about a Lower East Side troll that I had modeled entirely on Martin Millar's obscure novel *The Good Fairies of New York*. There was a god-awful variation of Tennessee Williams's "Desire and the Black Masseur" set in a prison, in which I was trying to write my way into an emotionally justifiable murder by cannibalism with erotic overtones. And the only other one I remember distinctly, of ten similar stories, was a bleak, barely fictionalized account of the time I ran away from home when I was fifteen and ended up snorting heroin for a hazy week with a lunatic named Guy in a gaudy suburb on the French Riviera.

My first-choice thesis advisor was on sabbatical and my second choice agreed to work with me only on the condition that I wasn't writing anything "too Southern Gothic, adolescent, or fantastical." I assured him I wasn't, and then went home and got writer's block. I decided that I had probably talked myself into a crisis and quite methodically went about trying to talk myself back out of it. I went to Health Services and asked them to refer me to a shrink who worked on a sliding scale. I requested someone who understood the writer's process. I wanted a woman who was older than me and smarter. Someone who talked—I loathed the idea of returning to a reticent man in a frumpy jacket, stirring rarely like an old turtle and just enough to ask me how that made me feel. I preferred a European Jewish intellectual.

I was quite specifically looking for a mother figure.

They referred me to Dr. Sondra Wilk, who, among other specialties, treated Juilliard students suffering stage fright. My mother had studied at Juilliard in the late 1950s. The bond I felt intuitively was forged as if by destiny.

A FRIEND OF mine once referred to the Upper West Side as the Boulevard of Dashed Hopes because of the high concentration of mental health professionals practicing there. Doctor Wilk's office was out of a Viennese film set. It was a cavern of a room on the second floor of a teaching institute with a chandelier lobby and a marble stairway. Her office was painted a deep purplish red and lined with bookshelves. The titles alone could have constituted an associative therapy. "What caught your attention?" she would ask if I broke off in the middle of a sentence, obviously distracted by a book on the shelf. "What's object relations?" I'd ask. "What's a 'refrigerator mother'?" Often I'd get stuck on something I just wanted to read: Jung on storytelling in Freud. *The Art of Loving. Escape from Freedom.* She'd sometimes offer to lend me the book I was interested in, but I never accepted, terrified that I'd forget to bring it back because I always forget to bring books back. The only book she ever talked me into borrowing was R. D. Laing's *Knots*—a frustrating book, written in verse about people too stuck in their emotional logic to extricate themselves from painful patterns. She very deliberately showed me that she had two identical copies, so I relented and borrowed it, and I still have it. Right here.

She was a diminutive person; her sweet little face practically disappeared under a formidable copper-colored Jacqueline Susann bouffant and glamorous pair of oversized sunglasses that she wore all the time, despite the fact that we met in the evening in her half-lit mahogany office. Every now and then, she'd take off the glasses to rub her eyes or wipe up a stray tear, revealing full eye makeup, opalescent gray eye shadow and thickly applied kohl and mascara. Maybe she didn't wear the sunglasses all the time, because what I remember so keenly are her pale eyes, under all that decoration, intent on mine, utterly unwavering. We'd face each other over her massive desk, piled high with everything imaginable—crystal paperweights, candles, moisturizer, a grand-looking rare wood Kleenex caddy, papers, folders, a plant that didn't need daylight, and a miniature teddy bear holding a toothbrush. I sat on a comfortable Victorian upright side chair. She sat in a huge leather wing chair, propped up by a carefully constructed system of pillows in order to ease an assortment of debilitating backaches. Even though I knew she was in pain a great deal of the time, I could never come around to thinking of her as a person with a body.

Doctor Wilk once told me about a patient who'd complained to her that the messy piles all over her desk—so out of his control— made him especially anxious. (It *was* chaos and she was always patting around in the piles, mouse-like, looking for a pencil.) Her response to him was to sweep the entire mess off the desk and onto the floor. In the story, her nonexistent body was fierce, unfurling to height like a snake, jewel-toned scarves and embroidered tunics whipping around her form in the tornado of her movement. Standing dramatically in the middle of the Dresden reenactment on her Oriental carpet, she pointed to her glossy clear desktop and asked him, "Is that better?"

AT OUR FIRST meeting, she asked me, as therapists do, to review my life story, just so we'd have somewhere to start. I reminded her I had come to her to get through my writer's block and she should know from the get-go that I had already worked out my mother issues—my mother and I had basically spent my college years intently repairing our relationship from the emotional damage we both sustained at each other's hands during my adolescence. Doctor Wilk listened attentively and scribbled notes in pencil on a legal pad—it would be the only time that I ever saw her take notes during a session. In fact, whenever Doctor Wilk opened my patient file—usually in an illustrative gesture—all I ever saw in there were those same three or four pieces of yellow paper, torn from the legal pad the first time we met.

It was a familiar, hackneyed narrative. One that I'd been through many times, a string of significant markers, a timeline of defining events. I was plowing along when something unexpected tripped me up—none of the usual drama, the divorce, the move from bucolic Texas, the running away from France, or my expulsion from the house the week of my seventeenth birthday. No, I got stuck talking about my high school graduation. I don't even know why it came up. It wasn't one of my regular getting-to-know-you stories. It wasn't even a story. It was just the end of high school, the day I walked down a grassy aisle, barefoot, my red graduation robes knotted cleverly along the hem to form an asymmetrical bell shape, and received an empty diploma case (I still had credits to make up), tossed my hat, and watched the crowds disperse, all of my very closest friends disappearing into clusters of family off to fancy lunches at Legal Sea Foods or the Beekman Arms. I might have considered—as I stood in the parking lot watching everyone leave—that for all of our camaraderie and manipulated adolescent Sturm und Drang, even my friends who'd been grounded, had their dressers searched for drugs, had routinely cut class with me, and also were receiving empty diploma tubes were nonetheless being gathered up by loved ones. I may well have been the only one whose family drama left me to stand by myself in a vacant auxiliary parking lot (soccer field). I let them all go, and then, alone, climbed into my pea green 1972 Buick Skylark that gave you an electrical shock during rainstorms, and drove away too.

It was, I found as I recounted it in Doctor Wilk's office, the saddest non-story I'd ever told. The non-story most emblematic of my teenage years—yet another clamorous failure that had no audience. I broke down, weeping as if for the first time. Doctor Wilk unwedged a stray Kleenex from a pile of strewn papers and file folders and pushed it across the desk toward me. She made notes on her legal pad, and then gently told me that we could finish the rest of my narrative at our next meeting.

Which we didn't do. My narrative was, by tacit accord, *complete enough* for therapy to commence. For the next five years I saw Doctor Wilk continuously, and she would frequently refer to my graduation day. I'd be frustrated at myself, or confused as to why this or that happened or why I responded to this or that in one way or another, and she would softly remind me that I was "the little girl who no one came to see graduate from high school."

WE ALL HAVE totemic stories. The way we choose them—and then choose to tell them—is more important ultimately than the actual events. Like historians, we all build significance into sequential events, whether they are random or clearly a formulation of cause and effect.

Here is another totemic story from much, *much* later, sometime in early 2005. I am thirty-five years old. My mother and I are in the oncologist's office of Brigham and Women's Hospital in Brookline, Massachusetts. I live in New York so I haven't been there to take her to every chemotherapy session, but I've always tried to find a way to be at meetings with the doctor if I can. It's a way of offsetting my mother's inability to fully absorb and then accurately report the doctor's recommendations, as well as her own inability to tell the doctor everything that's been on her mind.

"Any other questions?" offers the doctor. Because we're talking about the treatments that we're running out of.

"I was wondering whether you could just give me a quick run-down of Mom's record?" I ask unexpectedly. "I've gotten a little confused about the whens and the whats of the surgeries, chemo, radiation, and so forth over the last decade." My tone is glib, sort of aggressively frank. But I am using the term "decade" artfully.

The doctor has her game face on, and my mother is flipping through an old *Atlantic Monthly*, trying to divest herself of as much responsibility as possible for the appointment. Both of us are psychotically tired from having spent the weekend in the emergency room. She has bleeding lesions all over her chest, which she won't let the oncologist look at because they disagree about the diagnosis. My mother insists that they're burns from something called radiation recall, the doctor thinks it's the breast cancer metastasized to her skin. Whatever the diagnosis, my mother has to go to the Burn Center twice a week to have the wounds treated and dressed.

The doctor nods and spins around on her rolling stool to face the computer, which looks like it might have been purchased from Radio Shack the year the Go-Go's went platinum. After plugging in some codes, and scrolling down some screens, the doctor turns to me and starts, "Well, if we don't count the early diagnosis of breast cancer in 1991 that your mother didn't want to treat..."

I blink knowingly, as if to say, "Oh yes, that. I know all about that."

"The lymphoma diagnosis was in 1995 and we started the first chemotherapy in 1996."

What I remember distinctly from that moment was realizing that my mother actually had had cancer, of one form or another—because she battled three separate cancers—for more than a *decade*, not even counting the first diagnosis. All together it was a preposterously long time to have cancer. The duration had become as ferocious as the disease. What I didn't realize until now, *this* moment, tracking my own timeline, was that the year I started therapy for writer's block was the year my mother started chemotherapy. Self-delusion is a steely logician. I needed therapy from a mother figure, because I couldn't write. Because—in my messianic delusion—my mother's life depended on it.

IN THERAPY OR out of it, creating a narrative is a process. The first stage is a highlight reel, filled with Freudian reductions, one-liners, and clichés: I think, for example, of the way my mother described the grandfather she barely knew. He was a philandering, vegetarian pediatrician, who cheated on my great-grandmother Frieda with her best friend from the shtetl. And even though he'd left Frieda, he followed her and their children to America, periodically dropping into my mother's life despite being under strict orders to stay away—a phone call when she was sixteen, a letter when I was born suggesting that she name me after the best friend from the shtetl. Somehow this irresponsible jackal of a man ended up teaching pediatric medicine in Pittsburgh and was beloved by his students. One of those students somehow befriended my parents and it was in the garden of that student's house in Pittsburgh that I took my first steps. *Do I remember* how green the day lily leaves were? The flagstones solid beneath my feet?

After the highlight reel, you move into the chronology—to establish context—which is something like being hit on the back of the head with a five-pound bag of Idaho potatoes. Chronology is dull, deadly dull, and apparently infinite. The minutes of your life are so many, and how do you determine which minute is the minute that caused the minute that led to the incident of relevance? What's worse, the minutes of your life don't begin with your birth but with your genesis, which extends back past your conception, past your parents, back even to the shtetl. And how many minutes ago was that?

LIKE ME, MY mother didn't really do well as a student or even graduate high school. She didn't pass math, and she blew off the graduation ceremony. My mother didn't need her high school diploma because she'd already been accepted into Juilliard. She was going to marry a handsome film editor whom she would follow to New York City and then leave a year later for a handsome Norwegian composer who was married anyway and only in New York on a yearlong travel grant. All of which I learned the long afternoon I had decided to interview her, thinking a chapter about her would be a nice complement to the book I was writing about my father—having definitively abandoned fiction ten years earlier, the moment after I delivered my horrendous thesis. We sat down with a tape recorder and I asked her about her spirituality and what she remembered about her mother's life story, and she told me about love and about regret and regret and regret. It was *her* personal history, more candid and comprehensive than any she'd ever told before. It was, after all, for the record.

I never listened to the tape. I wrote my chapter without referring to it once, and plowed forward another year, writing and researching, interviewing, synthesizing and writing. Until I had finished a first full draft of my book. *Her* chapter, "Truancy," was the third. It started with a description of my mother that likened her to the sweeping arches of a Romanesque church, the pale stones lit to a golden hue by the afternoon sun streaming in through a rosette window set high in the wall.

She was aesthetic to a fault and I was tyrannically pragmatic. She'd arrange plants in pots that didn't quite fit, so they would teeter but they looked lovely. She would balance unusual plates and odd bits of glass on the mantelpiece as decoration. The whole house shook and clattered treacherously when you walked through a room. Her solution was that everyone should walk more carefully. Mine was to put the dishes away in the dish cabinet and take them out to eat off of them. We locked horns when I turned thirteen, the way mothers and daughters do. She was stunned. She was wounded. Her own mother had died when she was only thirteen. Teenagers, she thought, grieve. They long to have their mothers beside them again. She was only half wrong.

Rebelling against my mother was horrific. It was like punching a cat. We retreated from each other in shock. Absent, truant. The chapter about her ended with my high school graduation.

I put that first momentous draft into a massive black binder, with colored tab dividers marking each section. It was Christmas when I finished. I was alone in my mother's decrepit house in Tuscany, where my then-fiancé and I had gone to write our books. For the holidays, he was back in the States seeing family—and my mother was coming to visit. It was a rare pilgrimage for her, as the house was barely winterized and she usually stayed in it during the summer. To prepare for her visit I turned on all the space heaters, piled blankets on her bed, and laid in a store of propane tanks so that we'd have warm water.

The very first night after she arrived we decided to make giant stuffed artichokes, filled with chopped garlic and chopped parsley, chopped pancetta, and chopped artichoke hearts—just the way she used to have them when *she* lived in Italy as a young woman. I was so anxious about the book, the first draft of the first book I'd ever written, that I handed it to her the moment she arrived. "You read," I said. "I'll chop."

She sat on the couch to read while I worked mutely at the counter, my back to her, in that small, dim, chilly kitchen. She was so tiny and the binder was so big, I could hear the paper rustling violently every time she turned a page.

Stuffed artichokes are an extremely labor-intensive meal. I must have been working away at them for over half an hour when I realized with a start that it had grown deafeningly silent in the room. I hunched my shoulders as if expecting a blow from behind, because I knew somehow that she'd gotten to Chapter Three. I turned slowly to face her, the long chef's knife still in my hand.

She was sitting, her face turned down toward the binder, which she held closed in her lap. I didn't breathe because that would have broken the silence.

"Minna," she said. "I was there. I went to your graduation. But I hid so you wouldn't see me, because I thought you didn't want me there. I didn't want you to get mad."

ABOUT A MONTH before my mother died, she called me over to her side and said, "If they call, I don't want to talk to them." I pressed her: Who them? Why? Her hearing had gotten very poor, she felt that her brain had shrunk away from her eardrum and that all the people sounded like distant raspy ghosts. When people called, she worried that her life force might get sucked into the receiver to fill the chasm between the people and her ear. I realized then that my mother had already left me. We'd already had our last conversation. She had slipped away and we were holding vigil over her body, just trying to keep fear at bay.

Grief begins long before our loved ones die, the hospice nurse told me. For some, she said, death can even be the end of grief. Fifteen years earlier, I had been with my mother at the appointment in which her doctor told her that they'd found precancerous cells in her breast. The fear had started then. But when did my grieving start? When did the disconnect between dread and certainty start, the sense that I wasn't living entirely in my body, that there wasn't any part of this domineering cycle that could be controlled, and that my mother's life force *would* be violently sucked away? And yet, once she wasn't dying anymore but gone, once all the delusions were finally dispelled, once I didn't have the architecture of grief and fear to shape my life around, that's when things would start to get really bad.

Driftwood, Off the Record

Joey and I moved in together because we were very young and alone in Boston, which is basically an unfriendly city. I was just out of high school. Joey was marooned in his mid-twenties, a third of the way through music school, working fifty hours a week as a flower delivery guy for a family of brothers whose father had a made a fortune off his seat on the Dutch flower market. Two of the brothers weren't even as old as Joey—but that never bothered Joey as much as it bothered me on his behalf. I worked in the flower store too, taking telephone orders in the back of the Newbury Street location, and I got to work the floor one day a week. That was more fun but didn't pay as much.

We had a nice one-bedroom—wood floors and bay windows— we couldn't afford. It was on Pembroke Street in the South End, which was tree lined and still considered a little sketchy even though it was on the verge of gentrification. We ate economically:

ramen, mac and cheese, peanut butter sandwiches, and sometimes chicken, which I wore rubber gloves to prepare because the only thing grosser than meat is raw meat. Once a week we'd go out to dinner at the Claddagh, an Irish steak pub off Columbus, with green banquettes in the back room and drunk cops in the front.

It was a tiny world. We socialized mostly with Max and Liam, a wealthy middle-aged Australian couple. One blond, one bald. Max was an investment banker and Liam ran a ran a boutique PR company business. They both talked like Crocodile Dundee, and looked like my friends' fathers—but had more panache. Joey had met them through the Forum and rented a room from them until we moved in together. The Forum is rebranded second-generation est, the sadistic 1970s self-improvement program of workshops, encounters, master classes, and homework. Joey kept a stack of Forum homework worksheets on a clipboard—emotionally loaded self-assessment quizzes that he sweated over.

There were always young boys in the background at Max and Liam's designer apartment, crashed on the couch or sneaking daintily out of the bathroom in a towel. They were a barometer of where Max and Liam were on the self-improvement/dissolution spectrum. If there was only one boy and he was pretty, that was an upswing. Multiple boys, or boys who looked mangy and strung out, meant that Max and Liam were in a bad place—the carpet needed vacuuming, Liam couldn't stop yawning, Max's eyes looked melted and he would forget to be witty.

They were devoted to Joey, who, with his Levis, cheap leather jacket, owl-shaped glasses, and shaggy hair, couldn't have been less fabulous. Joey was an unreconstructed townie. He even looked like a rube at the Claddagh. He called sex "choking the chicken" and we did it standing up a lot—because we were kids and we could.

We didn't have a lot of furniture in our apartment. We never would. Some frying pans and the futon couch. I'd fashioned a desk out of milk crates and a hollow-core door I plastered over with photocopies of my face and dismantled lines from a Langston Hughes poem.

Love is a wild wonder
And stars that sing,
Rocks that burst asunder
And mountains that take wing.

John Henry with his hammer
Makes a little spark.
That little spark is love
Dying in the dark.

I was taking night classes at Harvard Extension School, and the desk was where I was supposed to be doing my Human Rights in Latin America homework, but mostly I fiddled with my pencils and drew word clouds in an oversized sketchbook. Joey was a musician so he had a keyboard, and a clipboard instead of a desk. When he played songs on his guitar he put on a fake whiskey voice that kind of embarrassed me and was also kind of endearing. Sometimes I'd come home to find him wearing his giant studio headphones and crooning tunelessly into his keyboard. I was never entirely sure he even wanted to be a musician.

Joey was hypoglycemic and whenever we'd have a bad day or a rare disagreement he'd buy two pints of Häagen-Dazs Vanilla Swiss Almond and eat them both from the carton while standing over the sink. Then he'd weave and slur around the apartment for fifteen minutes before passing out diagonally on the bed, his already bent glasses askew on his forehead and one hand down his pants. We didn't talk about the whole Forum thing too much because I thought it was a total mind-sucking sham and Joey felt like he was in a good place.

Joey had grown up in Westerly, one street over from the town beach. He had a motorcycle that he didn't want to keep in the city, so we took it out whenever we were in Rhode Island for the weekend. No matter what else was going on, that motorcycle was Joey's great redemption. I loved riding it along the shore roads. Who wouldn't? There was one steep bridge with a corrugated steel deck. The surface had no grip and riding over it was like hydroplaning on gravel. Add the wind off the ocean and the fog. The way Joey's body tensed up when we hit the bridge was the opposite of reassuring.

On the far side of the bridge, there was a little beach diner with lemonade and chili dogs that stayed open in the off-season. The diner was more of a shack and there were only three dingy tables and a sandwich counter inside. The main attraction wasn't the hot dogs but that it was where Joey always used to go with his friends back when he was in high school. The first time he took me, there was a blond kid behind the counter who I said looked like a "Stevie" to me. "Hey, Stevie?" I said.

"What can I do for you?" he answered, wiping his hands on his apron.

Things like that happened to me every so often and Joey would turn to look at me, his eyes wet with love.

He wasn't as besotted by the way I set up the answering machine. He had ideas about things making sense and I liked to challenge received ideas about what makes sense. Our outgoing message was a rap that I'd composed in my sketchbook:

You think you're lucky you've got a phone
But look what happens when you phone our home
We ain't clean but we got this machine
You have the choice now record your voice
Like you don't know already, you wait for the tone
Leave your name, your number, or a cosmic groan
Minna is grateful for the opportunity to talk to you though not
*   personally*
So now it's your time, say your say, and take our wishes for a very
*   nice day*

Answering machines in general confused Joey's mother. My rap on our answering machine put her over the edge. We'd come home, press the button to listen to our messages, and hear Joey's mother's voice, trembling with fear and uncertainty. "Hello?" she'd ask, the question mark echoing out over the wood floors. "Joey? Are you there?" A long silence and then she'd continue, "Can you hear me? Joey?"

Joey's father was an environmental engineer—a lifetime civil servant and a master gardener, which I learned was an actual accreditation. He was gentle, extremely smart, and very tall, unfolded-paper-clip tall. He still lived in the small bungalow that Joey had grown up in and when we stayed there, he'd take me on tours of his tiny, lush garden, explaining to me again and again how hydrangeas were naturally occurring blue near the ocean, and detailing his elaborate schemes for keeping the deer away from his just-ripe blackberries. Joey and his dad would sometimes joke that the toxic runoff from the town sewage plant was especially good for blue hydrangeas and thorny roses.

Joey's mother was more of a chore. She lived in an even smaller bungalow right next door with her infirm mother-in-law. It was a gloomy house, hidden from the road by a cluster of trees. Inside it smelled like furniture polish and urine. Joey's parents hadn't spoken in fifteen years when I met him but lived within spitting distance of each other. She didn't have hobbies and openly resented being left to care for the old woman; she was bored and miserable.

My parents didn't talk either. But at least they had the decency to not talk from different states. Joey's parents didn't talk from across a yard. The chasm seemed so much bigger that way. I remember Joey trying to explain it to me, but we didn't get very far. He wasn't a big storyteller.

Which seemed related to the Forum. In the Forum they worked on shaking out "the story we tell" from what actually happened, on the perfectly sound premise that if you tell the same story enough times, it hardens and becomes fact rather than raw experience. More important, your perspective on the story hardens too. So you find yourself twenty years down the line talking about and thinking about your parents' divorce as if you were still nine and it had just happened.

In Forum language: "When we are able to separate what happened from our story or interpretation, we discover that much of what we considered already determined may in fact not be that way. Situations that may have been challenging or difficult become fluid and open to change. We find ourselves no longer limited by a finite set of options, and able to achieve what we want with new ease and enjoyment."

In the Forum, telling stories is the opiate that subdues the masses. The self-deception that keeps the individual trapped in a bubble bath of low expectations. It's the inverse of Joan Didion's "We tell ourselves stories in order to live"—by which she meant, to survive.

I think we tell stories in order to relate, in order to find a point of communion with our fellow person, in order to say: Look, I get you. I've had this experience that's like your experience. So I get you. Do you get me? Because what's really key about me getting you is that you get me.

No one who is telling you a story is trying to be alone.

IT'S RELEVANT THEN to say at the outset that I haven't told this story before. Which means I don't have a predetermined idea about how it's significant. Which means, in my case, that it's a memory that either frightens or shames me. Which means it's an experience that I've never thought to draw upon to align me with another person. Not having told this story before means I never fixed many details in my memory and have to rely on flashes, the transparent stills that hang in my mind, made of smell, the way the light casts, the wind on skin. The big old gas-guzzling town car with the pearl gray leather seats, all the windows open, speeding down I-95 at dusk. The next exit is the one I take to get to the South Shore Mental Health facility, North Kingston branch. For a loony bin, it's surprisingly close to the highway.

[STORY]

We got a call. Something was wrong with Joey's mother and he had to go down and help. She had been found in a catatonic state, standing nonresponsive in the corner of the dining room, by the china cabinet, near the window but not looking out of it. We think she had been immobile in that position for days. She'd gone to the bathroom on herself. Joey's elderly grandmother had been stranded in the upstairs bedroom. Thank God she had a phone. I will forever conflate the image of Audrey Prescott in the corner, a pale lumpy form, those entirely blank eyes, with the plaintive voice recorded on our answering machine: *Are you there, Joey? Is anyone there?*

She was hospitalized and then committed. The diagnosis was astonishing. Joey's mother's brain had shrunk. They thought it was "housewife" drugs from the sixties: benzos and diet pills. Her brain was knocking around in her skull, like a marble in an empty cat dish. They couldn't exactly fatten her brain back up but they were hopeful that they could hydrate it a little so that it would get bouncier, more responsive. (I tried just now to research "brain shrinkage" in order to describe Joey's mother's condition more accurately. As a side effect of housewife-drug abuse, brain shrinkage per se does not appear to exist in the Internet age.)

We went into crisis mode, with Joey driving down to Kingston a lot and eating too much Vanilla Swiss Almond. I avoided going to the hospital because Joey's mother made me feel uncomfortable and helpless. I tried to be supportive at home.

"Stop eating all that fucking ice cream!" I said very loudly one night. For me, it was like an experiment in being emotional. "You'll get diabetes like your father."

"I don't fucking care," he answered, and then disappeared out the door for hours—which I think was Joey's lone experiment with being dramatic. It was like an unrehearsed scene from a movie. Everything seemed like it was from a movie when I was nineteen. Drama can be seductive until its consequences start piling up.

One of the times I didn't go with Joey to the asylum I went out to dinner with my mother and my sister instead. My mother wanted to "talk to us." Restaurant dinners with my mother (not including pizza or Thursday night Chinese) have always been events, and reserved only for the most shattering life announcements. This dinner was high theatrics before it started because I'd been essentially summoned from exile to attend.

My mother was the opposite of Joey's mother. The opposite of blank. *Her* pale blue eyes were restless with romance and regret. She was the opposite of catatonic; she was a raw nerve. She jumped when the wind moved the tiny curls over her ear. Nothing confused her—everything either intrigued her or terrified her. She thought my telephone rap was hilarious.

"I have found a miracle," she announced fervidly that night. "It's in a pill."

She'd started seeing a grief counselor at the college health clinic. Something she'd decided to explore when, a year after her stepmother's death, two years after her father's death, nine years after her divorce, she still felt inadequate to the task of daily life. "It's called Prozac," she explained. "I feel wonderful," she said. "I'm going to get better," she promised.

It was the summer of 1989. Barely a year and a half had passed since Prozac had been introduced to the American marketplace. The next spring, *Newsweek* would declare it the pill of the year. The cover of that issue would feature a giant Prozac hovering powerfully above a wasted cartoon desert-scape. The headline: "A BREAKTHROUGH DRUG." This was all before the news came out about Prozac triggering manic episodes, leading to suicide in young people, turning you into Elizabeth Wurtzel. But in this moment, at this dinner, Prozac was still only a news story that we'd heard in the background on the radio once. "Will you get addicted?" my sister wanted to know. "How do they know you have *depression*?" I wanted to know. I was probably thinking deep within myself, *You're just weak.*

"I don't have *depression*," she answered. "But I feel so much better."

I might have been out in the world, acting like an adult, but I wasn't one. What I comprehended—my "narrative"—was that my mother was a destructive femme fatale whose weapons were guilt and manipulation. She'd forced me into a shabby tough-girl masquerade and I wanted her to take me back, back in time to bedrooms with colored quilts and ceramic lamps and books I'd read fifteen times. It was my paradox. Mine. And yet there was a world of things I didn't understand. I didn't understand what she was saying to us. I didn't understand that alienation and depression are psychotic lovers, suck-locked together in a dark, caustic force field. I couldn't absorb her elation. I didn't understand the announcement or how it meant that everything would change now. I left the dinner worried that my mother was acting crazy, potentially an addict, and that her beautiful brain would shrink. And start rattling around in her skull like a marble in a cat dish.

WEEKS PASSED AND I began referring to this as the Summer We Committed Joey's Mother. And then one day Joey had a surprise for me but I'd have to brave a trip to the asylum in order to collect. He could barely contain himself. He led me through the towering sun-battled lobby into his mother's hospital room as if he were leading me into a surprise party. There was his mother sitting brightly up in bed, smiling joyously. Sitting beside her—beaming, lanky, and perfect somehow—was Joey's father.

You know that children of divorce dream of their parents' reconciliation. Maybe not every last one but a vast, unrealistic majority of us do. It's documented in an official landmark twenty-five-year study of children whose parents divorced in 1979. I have the data. I am the data. Joey was one of the exceptions. If he'd ever dreamed of his parents getting back together, he kept it hidden deeply away.

But he was giddy the day he let me know that his parents had been brought back together by his mother's grotesque episode, by her total neediness. His parents too were giddy, sitting together holding hands over the hospital sheets. It happens, I thought. I'm witnessing a miracle. They forgive each other. They go back to where they're supposed to be.

The next time I saw Joey's mother, she was in the kitchen of Joey's father's house, brightening it with happiness. She was dusting, plumping pillows, making eggs and a fruit cup. The ocean breeze was blowing so clean and rich through the open windows and doors. Joey's father was out back in the garden, whistling.

JOEY AND I had come together to take care of each other, to be orphans together. But then our parents started repairing. There was a boy from Italy I liked to have coffee with. For months, we'd meet in the Trident Cafe on Newbury Street. He'd smoke and I'd talk about art and we'd look at books. In a gesture of emotional perversion I will never entirely understand, I drove him down to Westerly one night. Perhaps I wanted him to see this beautiful place that was part of my life before it stopped being part of my life. There was a sudden summer downpour as we pulled into the parking lot of the town beach and I went tearing down to the dark shore, dancing heedlessly in the shallow waves and the rain. He grabbed me and kissed me. Lightning flashed across the sky and Westerly disappeared.

Joey and I parted lovingly; it was almost a relief. We packed up the apartment on Pembroke Street. I moved him back to Max and Liam's apartment and he moved me back into my mother's house. We'd see each other occasionally, even choke the chicken if the mood was right. Six months later he asked me for a ride down to Providence because his father had been in an accident. We hugged for fifteen minutes in the car before he headed into the hospital. I didn't go in with him because it wasn't my place anymore.

Joey's father had stepped on a piece of broken fencing while working in the garden. It was the fence he'd put up to keep out the deer even though he knew realistically that fences wouldn't deter them. The only way to protect the blackberries was to wake up before dusk and pick the ripe ones before the deer did. He was diabetic and got gangrene and lost his leg, his entire leg, up to his hip. I visited one day with Joey a few weeks after he'd gotten out of the hospital. He was a different man. Sitting on his porch, crutches cast off to the side, intentionally out of reach. He wouldn't look at us, kept his eyes on the horizon. Audrey was nearby calm and clear-eyed, because despite everything she was where she was supposed to be.

[EPILOGUE]

It was a while before I saw Joey again after that. It might have been a year. We met for dinner at an Ethiopian place on Mass Ave., on the Boston side near where he was living. Joey told me that he was happy. This is what he told me. He was working as a nurse's aide to a quadriplegic professor. In exchange for room and board and a small salary, he helped lift the professor in and out of the bathtub, got groceries, prepared food. He wasn't going to school anymore and had decided to take a break from the Forum. He was learning more, he thought, from the courage of the man he was living with. It wasn't an easy situation. Joey still had to work delivering flowers on the weekend shifts in order to make ends meet and the doctor had told him he had a herniated lumbar disk. He wasn't supposed to be lifting more than fifteen pounds.

"Like big flower arrangements?" I asked.

"Yeah, that's bad," he agreed.

"Or full-grown men," I said.

Distress Abandon

I blew six and a half hours yesterday ponging around Columbus Circle trying to get myself to the right lab with the right paperwork in order to get a blood test that will prove whether or not I have cancer. Yesterday was the Monday after Thanksgiving, which meant that I at once had a great deal of work to catch up on and no desire to be anywhere. Yesterday was also the day that my doctor was moving offices—from one building to another in the Columbus Circle zone—and didn't have telephone or computer service. The nurses and doctors could call out but I couldn't call in, to ask, say, where to find "the lab" that my doctor had referred to in a flurry of one-line e-mails over the weekend.

My doctor is a very popular and good doctor. He might leave you in the waiting room two hours, but he's the kind who then spends forty minutes with you. The fact that he's sometimes a guest on the *Today* show does not make me trust him less, or more, for that matter. I was primarily apprehensive, when I first met him,

about the fact of him being a man. It turns out that a male gyne-
cologist has the capacity to be concerned, even attentive, to matters that many women and their professional caretakers have been
indoctrinated to approach with gritted teeth, red wine, and sto-
icism. Chronic discomfort, for example, the suspicion of systemic
error, phantom aches, and debilitating pain, everything throbbing
or nauseating, off, discordant in the spheres. My doctor is attentive and says things like: *Well, there's nothing about it in the medical literature, but that doesn't mean it doesn't exist or can't happen! It
just means that nobody's written about it.* He writes prescriptions
for fabulous exotic drugs that have no side effects or that you can
only get in California, but as he scribbles, he'll note aloud that yoga
might work too—not dismissively, but just to remind you that if
you weren't as busy as you are, as neurotically, monomaniacally
selfless, you might feel better physically without the ketamine.
He's also in charge of some whopping percentage of Manhattan's high-risk pregnancies, which means that he's very busy with
babies being dangerously born and celebrities, and sometimes
it's very hard to figure out where I fit in. My babies are safely out
in the world; they go to second grade and kindergarten and have
colds and very painful paper cuts that require cartoon character
Band-Aids.

BECAUSE HE IS so busy my doctor showed me a few years ago how
to communicate with him via BlackBerry. Reaching him electron-
ically depends on concision. Subject line: *Bleeding Out.* Text box:
*Day 3. Weeping rash. Cramp pain = 8. Low fever. Ibuprofen helps. Tour-
niquet doesn't.* Allergies: *tree nuts, trout, dextromethorphan.* He has
to be able to read and comprehend all the salient points in one
glance on the miniature screen of his phone. You have three lines,
he told me. Don't add extra words. Think bullet points. So I go

surreal, try to channel Estragon from *Waiting for Godot* (he's pithy), telegraphing: *Something is more wrong than usual. Still.* [Looking wildly around as if the answer was inscribed in the landscape.] *I'm not pregnant.* He answers me by telling his assistant what to call in to the pharmacy and copying me on the e-mail. He has my last test results, which were irregular, and over the weekend when I transmitted an update he replied: *Blood test Monday.* Then he added a second line to his assistant that my panel should include the test that—I now know from the Internet—exists solely to detect a marker for ovarian cancer.

I waited a decent seventeen-hour interval before writing. Subject line: *Bloodwork Appointment.* Text: *I can't make an appointment on the weekend, should I just show up at your office Monday?* To which he replied: *No. The lab.*

Which brings me to Columbus Circle, an odyssey that wasn't the *Odyssey*. It was *Waiting for Godot*. Not knowing *where* the Lab was, nor feeling that it was appropriate to e-mail my doctor's emergency line for street directions, I decided to simply head to the vicinity of my doctor's office on Monday morning after dropping the kids off for school, and start my hunt there. When earlier that morning my son lobbied to stay home sick, this morning of all mornings, because of a cold, I panicked. I had a one-day window to take this test; if I missed it I'd have to wait another month, which I arbitrarily decided could be fatal. I told him impatiently that people didn't skip school for colds. People felt rotten for colds, but they took Tylenol and soldiered through the day. Which made him cry. He felt like a swollen infected slug, not a soldier of endurance. And he was right. My own head throbbed dully in sympathy. I either had cancer or had caught his cold, and the best course of action would be a long day on the couch with ginger ale and chicken soup. Except I haven't had a long sick day on the couch since I was in elementary school; and I had to manually override the hysteria switch that would have had me engaging him in a battle about whose symptoms should take priority that morning. One of the symptoms of my illness is a hormonal imbalance that turns me into a raging, weeping histrionic with constant indigestion. And I'd like nothing more than to have this all resolved so that I can listen without tears to *All Things Considered* on my afternoon commute.

ESTRAGON: What exactly did we ask him for? VLADIMIR: Were you not there? ESTRAGON: I can't have been listening. VLADIMIR: Oh . . . Nothing very definite. ESTRAGON: A kind of prayer.

I LINGER IN my daughter's kindergarten classroom to watch Selina, one of the parents, read aloud from her book *Daddy Christmas and Hanukkah Mama*. I love watching the children in their morning meeting. They all have questions: "Daddy found a worm on the sidewalk and cut it with a shovel and the two parts were still living." "My brother wants a Christmas tree but it's too early because the cats will knock it over." "We have a tree." "How did you write that book?" My daughter's hand has been in the air for so long that she has to hold her right arm up with her left. She is dying to tell Selina about the book that *she* wrote over the weekend. It's called *Birthday My Party*. I realize I have to find Hanukkah presents and gelt for the kids sometime during the day. They have been keeping track of how many days I'm behind on presents—four—and they are very disappointed in me. I have made an unprecedented mess of Hanukkah.

IT'S NINE BY the time I leave the classroom and I have to retrace my footsteps home to get my phone, which I forgot. On my way from the house to the subway I call the doctor's office for the address to the

Lab. I get put through to the emergency answering service, which is when I learn that there is no way to contact the office because of the move. The operator does not know what lab my doctor uses but she takes my urgent message, which patently doesn't count as a medical emergency, and promises to try to get someone to call me back. Over the course of the hour-long subway ride, I become increasingly more embarrassed about having left such a message and increasingly scared that I won't get tested today and I'll have to wait another month. I've nervously sipped so much water on the ride that I head from the subway directly to the bathrooms at the Columbus Circle mall. From inside the stall I compose a lighthearted message to my doctor and his assistant. Subject line: *Where is the Lab?* Text: *Office closed can't get through. Just need address.* "Winter Wonderland" is blasting through the mall's sound system and I idly wonder whether they have gelt at Williams-Sonoma.

I CHECK GODIVA, Williams-Sonoma, and Whole Foods. No one has gelt. Upper West Side, New York City. There's an outrage in here somewhere. Alas, I realize, all the purchasing decisions for these uptown stores are being calibrated from Minnesota, where, I think, Hanukkah must be exotic—hardly something you program into your supply chain. An e-mail comes in from the doctor: *Phone number?*

FROM THIS MOMENT in the day onward, I will keep my phone in my right hand at all times. I avoid overpasses and stay out of the lower level of the mall. I cannot miss the phone call that will come and tell me where I'm supposed to go. I start prowling the stores as a distraction while I wait for the phone call, looking for Hanukkah presents. Sephora, J.Crew, Hugo Boss, L'Occitane. Nothing. My backpack is heavy with work, the Italian novel I was supposed to spend the day writing about before the medical crisis—but even if I could find a quiet place to sit down, I wouldn't be able to focus. Another hour of window shopping and my skin is creeping from the perfumed synthetic air. For the first time that day it occurs to me that there must be some kind of lab at the hospital three avenue blocks over, where my doctor attends, where my daughter was born, in fact, and maybe *that* is the Lab he meant. I make a beeline for the exit.

The instant I hit the fresh cool air of Fifty-ninth Street my composure disintegrates. I feel like a pod person race-walking down an ugly city block; as if whatever in the world might be grieving me is in fact irrelevant to the 1,700 people streaming around me. A group of classical music students are clustered by a bus kiosk. The largest of them, a bearded young man who looks like a trombone player, claps his hands in sudden excitement, the group laughs, his story escalates and he, a dancer now in this story, lurches backward, catches air. He's so large and so spontaneously mobile; his body spirited by the banter and laughter of his friends. When his elbow clocks the side of my head I see stars and gasp audibly. The group freezes; for a moment there is total silence and I feel great shame for having done that to them. They can plainly see that something is wrong. I whisper "That's okay" and back away. My phone rings.

ESTRAGON: A vague supplication. VLADIMIR: Exactly. ESTRA-GON: And what did he reply? VLADIMIR: That he'd see.

STRICTLY SPEAKING, THE nurse tells me, I've already missed my window to have this test done. I should have had it yesterday, Sunday. I crouch behind the stoop of a fire exit somewhere behind all the shops and tearfully remind the nurse that it's an "important test" and I don't think I can possibly wait. Her voice is full of compassion, but she'll need to ask the doctor. She'll have to call me back. I look down at my mother's wedding ring, which I had perversely slid on that morning for luck. It's a rosy gold and my mother had it made in Italy. She designed it herself because she never wanted anything to be the way everyone else had it. Instead of a band, she ordered an undulating wavy wobbly ring that always looks like it's on crooked. A perverse lucky charm: her marriage ended very sadly in divorce and then she spent fifteen years battling lung cancer and lymphoma before succumbing to breast cancer ten years ago this Thanksgiving.

"Why are you convinced you have to live your mother's life?" my therapist asks me, like clockwork, every two or three months. Sometimes it's her response to a comment I've made about my divorce or loneliness or parenting. Other times, she'll say it as a way to counter my cancer projections. "*When* I get my breast cancer," I will say. "How can you be so sure?" she'll answer. "Genetics," I'll say. "And temperament."

I'M NOT AS hidden by the stoop as I'd thought. I realize I might as well be crouched in the middle of the sidewalk and people walking past can see me, miserable, and cradling my cell phone. I worry someone might lean down and check on me to make sure I'm okay. Or worse, not.

When the nurse calls me back an hour later, I'm in H&M, standing in front of a faceless mannequin garishly dressed in a red Icelandic sweater and Christmas lights trying to figure out if I can pull off fake leather pants if it turns out I do have cancer.

I can get the test after all, she tells me, and we move on to the subject of the Lab. It turns out that there is no *the* Lab. People just have labs that they go to all the time, the way they have pharmacies they go to. You go to your lab and your doctor sends over a prescription. I don't have a regular lab but there is, it turns out, a lab right across the street from me—good thing I happen to be haunting the streets of Columbus Circle. I'm to go to the lab and, in fifteen minutes, the nurse will call and tell them to give me the blood test.

If you are a lab technician, or run a radiology practice front desk, even answer phones at a pharmacy, or work as a health insurance adjuster, you will have perceived already how terribly flawed our plan was. No one takes diagnostic test orders over the phone like Chinese food. But because cell phone signals are scrambled in the big concrete office building where the lab is, my nurse can't reach me in the lab waiting room (which is about as cozy, not incidentally, as a takeout Chinese restaurant) to tell me that the lab won't take me after all.

VLADIMIR: Charming evening we're having. ESTRAGON: Unforgettable. VLADIMIR: And it's not over. ESTRAGON: Apparently not. VLADIMIR: It's only beginning. ESTRAGON: It's awful.

So I SIT on the folding chair and watch Dr. Phil interview a woman whose father killed her mother and then hired his mistress to be the new nanny. Dr. Phil brought the nanny out onto the stage too, to confront the grief-stricken daughter. My hormones are so out of whack at this point, the nanny's story brings tears to my eyes. Thankfully the lab technician behind the bulletproof glass finally calls me over to reveal that she's talked to my nurse and my nurse can't charm her way into not providing an actual order for blood work. I need to walk over to the doctor's new office—which is a construction site three avenues away, past a gorgeous-smelling falafel truck and a five-story art store where I find Hanukkah Silly Putty, Hex Bugs, and a Peregrine Falcon action figure—and get the physical paper prescription from what will be the front desk of my doctor's new practice: the special cancer marker test, inhibin 1 ultrasensitive, carved into the triplicate form with a Bic, alongside the usual battery of thyroid tests, hormone panels, and iron levels.

CLASSIC DRAMATIC STORYTELLING structure would have a reckoning here, a reversal. I would have an epiphany and emerge from the squalid doctor's office out into the light, glowing with some higher understanding of life's insurmountable obstacles, and some veneer of reconciliation. I spent years waiting for my long dark night of the soul to end—to come to a riotous, triumphant conclusion. Is it here now? I'm fine but not fine. I can behave for the most part like the person I was but I am changed. Un-innocent. These descents into dark nights are murky—like *Waiting for Godot*. They don't end, reveal, or release us into bright inner peace. Quite the opposite. The characters are left staggering off the stage, alive to wait another day. It's a sad journey without a grail.

WHEN THE PHLEBOTOMIST in the Chinese takeout laboratory finally calls to me through the bulletproof windows, it is late in the afternoon. Another patient in the waiting room has just indignantly requested that we be allowed to turn off Dr. Phil. I'm so tired I think I'm numb; but when the needle pricks my skin, it stings, then burns. I feel an enormous relief. *Take it*, I think, giddily. *Take it all.*

Lapsus

I was introduced to the idea of Monica Sarsini this way: my college boyfriend, who was from Florence, said, "You have to meet my mother's friend. She's a writer. She's strange and beautiful. She's anorexic. She's agoraphobic. She lives downstairs. You should read her." He produced a slender book from his mother's jammed shelves. The title was *Crepapelle*. A nonsense word. With peculiar childlike pleasure, he went on to describe the book as a menagerie of fantastical hybrid animals. The dense, sonorous other-dimensional language was too difficult for me, with my remedial Italian, to read at that time. But I took the book away with me, and kept trying.

I was introduced to the *actual* Monica Sarsini shortly after, when she held an open studio in her living room to show a friend's paintings. She was beautiful and tiny, an exquisite skeleton. But unlike the haunted neurasthenic I had conjured from what I'd heard about her and from what I'd read in her words, she was sunlight—laughing loudly, mouth open, teeth flashing. She grabbed both my hands firmly, fixed her face to mine, and told me that she was absolutely delighted to meet me. I was nineteen and she embodied feminine perfection. Large black eyes, heavily lined with kohl, cheekbones like bird wings, thick black hair pinned in a messy upsweep. She wore high-heeled boots (always) but didn't teeter. She clomped and stood her ground. She was ferocious, not sickly. It was months before I worked up the courage to speak in her presence.

After we'd grown close—once I'd recovered my tongue—she told me about books. In particular she introduced me to Thomas Bernhard, who was her hero. She gave me *Gargoyles* and described the dark gloomy landscape, the trepidation of the child's perspective. She allowed that it was a singularly depressing book, even though she loved Bernhard mostly because he was such a hoot, albeit a grumpy hoot, exquisitely mean. Despite being a firmly established figure in the tiny Florentine art scene, Monica was always deeply insecure about her art, and she easily saw herself in his stern outlier sensibility. She told me the story of how she'd met him in 1982, when he came to Florence to accept the Premio Prato. He was reluctant to be there at all, and seemed, according to Monica, to have thought he could just come to the ceremony and collect the money. But they wanted to praise him at a fancy dinner; and they wanted him to say a few words. He begrudgingly approached the podium, looked out at the room of expensively coiffed cultural bankers, and muttered "Too terrible" in English. And then he left.

For years, I've imagined her as a full participant in that scene. I imagine her picking Bernhard up at the Florence train station in her wrecked Fiat 500. I imagine him folding himself into the tiny seat next to her, barely noticing the floors littered with cigarette butts, the backseats pulled out to make room for her colorful papier-mâché statues. I imagine them smoking Gauloises, the plumes wrapping Monica's bodacious laughter and curling out the open windows as the car peddled down the freeway, in the break-down lane, toward Prato.

The first full-length story of Monica's that I translated into English was a broad interior essay about a car ride. The piece is titled "Sunday" and in it she explains how difficult it had become for her to venture out of the small neighborhood in the center of Florence where she lived:

> *If my mother asks what I've decided to do today, I don't have it in me to answer that yet again she has thrown me into a state of panic; she beckons me and I can't come to her. I haven't been back to the countryside in years, and she doesn't seem to notice that I spend Christmases, birthdays, anydays without them all because they won't come to me; they wait for me to come, to meet them at the end of a road that I no longer know how to follow.*

In the story, her boyfriend's new sedan is fast, comfortable, and quiet. She looks out the window silently, watching the landscape fall past. They have lunch in a tavern, right at the foot of the hill where her family's country house sits. They visit a factory up the road from the country house. They while away the Sunday, but she remains unable to let him drive her up the dirt road to the country house, where her family spends Sunday without her.

Monica was never in fact agoraphobic. She didn't like to leave her neighborhood, where she knew everyone on the street by name except tourists, who didn't heavily frequent that quadrant of the city. She didn't like to be so far from her home that she couldn't retreat there in a few moments if panic were to seize her. But she wasn't afraid of open spaces, per se; she was afraid of one old farm-house, set on the slope of a mountainous hill, across the Arno, east of the city, halfway between the golden fields of Chianti and the ghostly pine forests of Vallombrosa. Her childhood home, Miransú. The name means "look up."

I didn't start seeing Monica regularly until my senior year of college. I'd decided to translate her stories as my senior honors thesis. I spent that winter break in Florence, seeing Monica every three days or so in order to work with her on the translations. We'd sit on her couch in her new apartment, just across the ring boulevard from her old apartment, for hours on end side by side, drinking sweet black coffee, smoking cigarettes, eating eggs poached in tomato sauce, parsing out twisted Italian syntaxes and discussing the meanings of words in tremendous deep detail. She was exacting about her word choice and wildly untamed in her grammar—a comma was a breath, a semicolon two, a period was a breath with a rest, and a new paragraph was a long breathless leap. We spent an hour discussing the word *feritoia*—the untranslatable title of one of her stories. A *feritoia* is a narrow vertical opening in the side of a fortress, slanted at just such an angle so that a soldier can see the enemy approach, or shoot an arrow or firearm, yet remain totally protected behind the thick stone wall. My translation dictionary offered "slit"—and we both knew that it wouldn't do. "*Feritoia* is defensive," she explained. "A position of power." Monica was hidden behind a *feritoia*.

When I defended my senior thesis, my panel said sympathetically, "How dreary." "How terrible for you," said my Dante professor, "to have to sit in this work for the last year." I flashed to the image of Monica next to me, confiding, laughing, her long narrow fingertips fluttering up to her collarbone. Monica's poetic writing was almost too complex—I had to translate it in order to parse it, interpret it, read it. "Not really," I told the panel. I had loved that year of trying to become someone else through language. I loved trying to understand a person through her words.

It was an honor that she had trusted me, so young, to translate her stories. "Broken Birds" was the thesis title I had settled on once I realized that I was still too inexpert a writer to do justice to the idiosyncratic wordplay of her real titles. An entire series of titles— "Crepapelle," "Crepapancia," "Crepacuore"—too precise for me to surrender to their English counterparts. *Crepa* means "to die"—a withering away kind of dying, but with slangy diction—"croak" . . . "kick bucket." Her titles were compound words that come out to something like: "Dead-Rot-Skin," "Dead-Rot-Belly," "Dead-Rot-Heart." Instead, "broken birds" was a single phrase lifted from the collection's central story, "Lapo."

At thirteen her older brother had been accidentally shot in the head by a neighbor boy, and when it happened, the family, her mother and father, collapsed, she wrote, around Lapo's hospital bed, like so many broken birds.

Lapo had died the day before Christmas. He'd been shot while climbing an olive tree in the grove that rolled down the slope from the old farmhouse that Monica was afraid to go to. By the time I came back to Italy after college, though, she had determined to overcome that fear and one day return to Miransú. She lived in a new house, even farther from the city center and the neighborhood where I'd first met her. She lived with her boyfriend in a single-floor apartment on a road leading out of the city toward the Etruscan hill town of Fiesole. The living room opened up onto a massive stone balcony overlooking the vineyards and olive groves of the great estate next door. Plunging herself into that provocative setting was part of a strategy to get back to the olive groves of her childhood.

Monica was always strategizing. I realize now that it was one of the most energetic components of her character. Days after I'd landed back in Florence, with a college degree in Italian literature and occasional part-time work affixing subtitles to movies to be shown at film festivals, Monica proposed that we go into business together. The local Communist Women's Center was inviting suggestions for evening courses, and she wanted to teach creative writing. I had ten pages of a teenage angst story and some critical theory as credentials. But, as Monica saw it, I'd taken two semesters of creative writing in college and so I knew how an American workshop ran. The fact that I still stumbled grotesquely when I spoke or, God forbid, wrote Italian was an incidental concern. All the confidence I lacked, Monica had tenfold on my behalf. She wanted me next to her; it was the only way she'd have the courage to do this. And we both needed money, she pointed out.

Yet again I was drawn reluctantly into a situation by the magnetic force of someone needing me. In this singular instance it was a total success. At that time, we were the only creative writing workshop in Italy. People came from great distances to study with us. There was a pharmacist from Pisa, an enlisted soldier from Bologna, a postal worker from Fiesole (who, for some urgent reason I can't recall, I convinced to read *The Spirit Catches You and You Fall Down* in English), and a bilingual Oxford graduate who wrote exquisite set pieces about her cat—sometimes mixing her two languages into her own private patois. Monica, with her reverberating laugh and bottomless stores of compassion, was the charismatic. Our students were happy; those two hours every Wednesday evening lifted people out of their lives, made them feel connected to something beyond pharmacies and barracks and postage, made them feel heard and important. That was Monica's great gift.

And then I decided to move to New York City to go to graduate school. Monica was angry at me in a way that I didn't quite absorb. I was young and cavalier and couldn't perceive her feelings for what they were. I didn't, in fact, understand them at all. My guilt was free-floating. My discomfort was chilling. I didn't understand that I was leaving her behind. I was going to "pursue writing" on some—albeit bogus—professional level. I'd adopted her home as my own but hadn't committed. I was going to New York when she couldn't even go to Pisa. I was flying away. I was young, twenty years younger, so I could just go if I wanted to. But the heart of the matter was that to Monica I was breaking a pact, a partnership, an intimacy that I had fallen into happily but by accident.

Every time for the next few years that I would come back for a visit—a summer or Christmas break—she would embrace me warmly and then we would sit together as if on a stage while she formally, sometimes snidely, inquired how my new life was going. She would increasingly crowd our visits with other friends, the permanent women of Florence: deeply politicized, smoky women with functional haircuts, expensive jewelry, and heavy bosoms. Under their auspices she kept the creative writing classes going. For the first year, she kept an empty chair beside her where I would have sat. Into the second year, she still billed the classes under both of our names.

We settled into a groove of love and almost open resentment. Monica would regularly send me her new work, asking me to translate it, to get it published. Meanwhile, the more deeply I implicated myself in the world of New York publishing, the shyer I felt about my work and I shared it less and less readily, while also being desperate to publish myself.

Six years passed. I decided with my boyfriend to move back again to Italy, to sit in the middle of the remotest end of Tuscany, in my mother's cramped, underheated house, live on olive oil and tomatoes, and write books.

There were three critical changes in this prodigal moment: First, I was bound like glue to this subsequent boyfriend, as I'd never been to a man before. Second, Monica adored him almost from the start and he also loved her—and so I had returned, at last, but the days of me and Monica, together alone, talking about books and writing were irretrievably past. Third, and perhaps most important, because it represented the end of one chapter and the beginning of another, Monica had, in the intervening years, made her way back to Miransú.

MONICA HAS BEEN a bell, ringing loudly at each station of my coming of age. And as absorbed as I've been with myself, or how she's felt about me, I haven't been able to see how our friendship reflects my passing. How I move through life like a dervish and she chimes from her fortified tower.

That November we all went together to pick olives at Miransú. I'd translated that house years earlier, building a picture of a place I'd never been through Monica's darkest and fondest memories. The grand stone kitchen with a fireplace you could almost stand up in. A heavy white curtain in the doorway to a living room that stands eternally waiting for Christmas morning. A wooden desk in a small sitting room with high ceilings and painted wooden furniture—the window that looks from there out over the stone driveway, and past that to the wickedly steep hillside, littered with fat ancient olive trees. The chicken coop out the side door; enormous vats of oil stacked to the side of the tractor garage with the caretaker's apartment above it. Large shallow wood-slated boxes, heavy with fresh olives—meticulously layered so that they wouldn't get squashed under their own weight. The air greasy with the peppery perfume of olive juice.

Picking olives with Monica and her family at Miransú was beautiful. She was there at last, and peaceful. She'd gathered all the courage she had to come back; and then once she'd made the leap, her heart blossomed. We were happy too. We worked hard and then feasted on bread blackened in the giant kitchen fireplace, rubbed with garlic and soaked in tangy fresh olive oil. Everything came together around a dark wooden table in a vast stone kitchen in a farmhouse on a hill in Tuscany.

That time, the last time, that I left Monica and Florence, I was on the cusp of real adulthood: my first book was about to be published, my boyfriend and I were going to be married, start a family. We said we would all come back soon and pick olives at Miransú. I haven't spoken again to Monica since I finished that book; since I married my boyfriend and then divorced him. The drama and anger. The missteps. She, more than almost anyone, knew me at my most idealistic, and I had failed her before I had even started failing myself. She hasn't met my children. She doesn't know where I live anymore. "Too terrible."

It's very easy to find pictures of Monica online. She's gotten involved with teaching writing to women prisoners, and an anthology she published of their work brought her a lot of attention. There are pictures of her presenting the book in the city's lavish library. She goes into schools and teaches writing and art to children. She teaches them how to make fantastical animals out of colored tissue paper, wire, and paste. There are pictures of her holding up their creations, her face lit up with delight at what children invent. It was a shock to see her, my image of her frozen a decade ago—maybe even a decade before that, when I first met her. She was my age then. Now she is sixty. My mind's picture of her has shattered. I would be ashamed to tell her how I've spun so far from her, from what she gave me, the trust she put in me, ashamed to recover that lost time.

Names Have Been Changed

People remember what they can live with
more often than how they lived.

—David Carr, *The Night of the Gun*

My boisterous children are lovable and brilliant. They travel well, sit still for manicures, they say things like "Mommy, I don't want you to waste your money on that." My baby girl has plump thighs, rosy cheeks, and curls just like Shirley Temple. She calls mascara "eye stylish" and wants to wear some too. My son is built like a reed. His hair is a sandy beach shag and his big brown eyes glimmer wetly with soulfulness. But my children, like all real children, have their dark sides.

My daughter is heavy; not fat but dense, uncomfortably dense. She is a medicine ball. She is poured concrete. I tried attachment parenting with her, I tried babywearing—which was supposed to make her confident, self-possessed, individuated—but her weight was too much and I got a hairline fracture on my left hip. So she is strong and confident, that is her nature, but she isn't individuated—she won't let me go. She clings to my limbs. If I sit down she climbs on my lap. If I kneel down she climbs on my legs. If I bend down she lunges, wraps her steel trap arms around my neck, and says "I want Mommy." She screams if I leave the room. She has a tantrum if I tell her to let Daddy brush her teeth. She punches her brother when he tells her, "This is a pretty dress you can wear today."

"I want Mommy," she howls as she watches blood stream from her brother's chin. All she wants is to be picked up and cuddled like a three-year-old, carried when she's tired, swept from the sidewalk when she falls. She wants to be a baby just a little longer but she's too heavy so she can't.

AT SIX YEARS old, my son is wound forty degrees past his breaking point. This is how it works. You say, "Time for dinner. Turn off the TV and wash your hands." He says, "Okay," and he gets up and turns off the TV and trips gaily into the bathroom to wash his hands. He returns just as gaily, flapping his damp hands in the air. He leans into his chair and asks, "What's for dinner?" You answer, "Bacon cheeseburgers," and in an instant his face crumples, a crescendo wail of agony moves from deep in his belly out through his mouth, nose, and ears too. He hurls his face down onto his arms and sobs.

"My darling," you say. "What in the world is the matter? There's bacon. There are cheeseburgers." He lifts his face up, it is vermillion, glistening with tears and snot, all flowing steadily down his chapped cheeks. "*That* is not what I *felt* like eating."

Revealing to him each morning that there is in fact school today provokes the same reaction. Revealing to him once in a blue moon that we have all spent the day together, eaten out, seen friends, gone to a street fair, picked apples, attended a birthday party, met a nice dog, played soccer, and bought him a harmonica at the toy store—and now it is bedtime, and there is no time for TV, provokes the same reaction. "But that's not *fair*," he weeps. "We *never* get to watch TV." I always rush to his side when he dissolves like that, cuddle him, beg him not to whine. I know that he is really crying because I divorced his father.

Assuming that at some point their skin will harden and not glow; their bodies will smell; they will not live here; they will not be able to confirm my pure, uncomplicated love for them every day. Assuming all of this injury that is sure to come, do you think it would be all right to write a memoir about them? I wouldn't use their real names?

Though even if I did, it wouldn't mean that you know them—or that I understand them yet myself. Someday they will blame me for mistakes I already can't undo. I can't write a memoir about them. I can only write my own stories, and hope that if I'm very careful, the only person you'll misunderstand is me.

I've realized definitively that every person's story is partial. By which I mean that every story leaves things out—a lot of things; there aren't enough pages in the world to hold everything. And by which I mean, it's subjective. I can only tell my version of my story. *That* means that everyone in my story is misrepresented. I've come to also understand definitively that there is nothing more terrorizing than being misrepresented, because its consequence is being misunderstood. There is nothing more agonizing in human relations than being misunderstood—your heart, intentions, aspirations, expressions, failings. There's no way that other people's stories, their versions of events, don't misunderstand you. "*Le langage est source de malentendus.*" All of the unsent love letters in my storage boxes are earnest, delirious, and incomprehensible attempts to explain myself.

As teenagers, I think we experience a unique (and somehow developmentally appropriate) claim on being misunderstood. I certainly did, and was. Yet I had the most exceptional curveball thrown at me right as I was entering the Hellmouth of adolescence: my mother took my sister and me away to Europe for her sabbatical year.

We first spent the summer in the South of France, staying in apartments that her college used during the year for their study abroad program. While we were there, we walked, ate, looked at fountains, and took French lessons at the local university. A friendly neighbor, one of the only people in the small town who spoke English, made a pass at me. "We don't have to tell my wife. We don't have to tell your parents." He was elderly by my standards. I was horrified and insulted, but also I felt betrayed—because upon our arrival the neighbor had, in his sturdy English, encouraged us to think of him as our guide. So late at night after his unwelcome overture, my sister and I, consumed with indignation, threw old fruit and eggs at his windows. He woke up and started screaming out the window that he was going to call the police. "I know who you are!" he shouted in English. We crouched and giggled sound-lessly against the wall below the open window in our dark apart-ment. We were homesteaders in the wild west, fending off the band of outlaws. Our pa's farm was all we had left.

The next morning, he went to our mother and complained. He insisted we apologize and clean up the mess. I refused to apologize, but I did get dressed up in my fanciest dress—a deep rose-colored silk with puffy sleeves that I'd worn to my sister's bat mitzvah—and armed with a bucket and sponge went down to the street below his window and scrubbed the sidewalk, singing loudly as I scrubbed, "Nobody Knows the Trouble I've Seen." My voice echoed prepos-terously through the tiny stone street.

MY MOTHER WANTED to spend this sabbatical year in Florence, Italy, because that was where she had lived as a young woman. She had lived one year there on a Fulbright to study with the great Modernist composer Luigi Dallapiccola. She fell in love and extended her stay, returning to her parents' home in Philadelphia only for a few months in the summer to earn money. She came back to Florence planning to get married and live there forever. But she'd met my father during that summer trip home and they'd fallen in love. He proposed to her by mail. She packed up her cat, Mozart, and returned to America to live there forever.

MY MOTHER WAS a Virgo. She arranged everything around her prettily, found organization in chaos and art in everything. She was stubborn but not overly concerned with proving herself to anyone but herself. She didn't follow rules; I don't even think she heard rules or knew that they applied. Her greatest battles were with herself—her emotions, body, behavior—and with us, her two daughters, by extension. Extension of herself. In the way she tended to narcissism, she tended not to separate the two of us from herself and her battles. Her love was fierce, almost romantic, uncomprehending, and greedy.

My mother was making it up as she went along. We drank powdered milk for the first eleven years of our lives, after which we converted to cream. She thought real milk was too fattening for us when we were small, but would pack butter sandwiches in my sister's lunch. Big greasy slabs of butter wedged between two slices of pumpernickel.

She didn't make friends with other parents, and I remember so often wishing she would because then (to my mind) she would understand better. She would know what was normal behavior for girls of our age. I suppose I was envious too of all the suburban houses with packaged snack foods and cable television. Kids who got clothes from department stores and belonged to soccer teams. I was convinced that it was a good idea to have a pantry stocked with canned goods in your finished basement in the event of nuclear holocaust. I probably liked the orderly plenitude of a good bomb shelter—so unlike our life of dust bunnies and hardwood floors, smelly cheeses, and old furniture.

ONCE UPON A time I had so many stories about my mother. I felt as if I were formed of them—things my mother did or said, ways I reacted, and how she reacted to my reactions—and it all seemed terribly broken and vital. Her mother died when she was thirteen, so what did she know about being a mother to teenage girls? She'd never had one herself. Now I'm a mother wondering what I know about being a mother and also making it up as I go along. Those stories don't hold the same sway over me that they once did. I no longer feel like I'm made out of her, or living in her footsteps or despite her footsteps. Now it's her absence that dominates.

AFTER THE SUMMER in France, we moved to Italy for the year. I started studying Italian at the American School of Florence. Almost instantaneously, I lost all of the handy French phrases I'd learned over the summer. I have no instinct for foreign languages, and could never run drills through conjugations and vocabulary the way you're supposed to. If a foreign language was ever going to make sense to me it would be because I understood it, not because I'd memorized some corresponding word. I abandoned the idea that I was going to learn Italian in class, or even at all. I found refuge in letting the world surround me, peacefully, incomprehensibly. In other words, I spent almost all of that year in Italy never speaking Italian. I just listened instead. I loved the way it sounded almost as much as I loved the green air of Tuscany, the hills, the ancient damp houses, and the way everyone talked to you whether you answered them or not. I loved being a foreigner, the constant sense of unfamiliarity that supplanted all of my expectations and disappointments. For a year, I didn't walk around with the bitter feeling that life wasn't what it was supposed to be. I didn't understand and I wasn't understood—or misunderstood.

That year, we lived in a little apartment over the chicken coop adjoining the barn of a vacated aristocratic property in Chianti. In addition to chickens, there were two large gray birds of a variety I'd never seen before. They tried to waddle away one morning while my sister and I were waiting for the bus that took us to school and the groundskeeper came running after them, shooing them off the road back toward the barn. "What are they?" my sister asked in her best schoolgirl Italian. "Ducks," he answered. "But they are dumb ducks. They don't know how to talk." Like me, I thought. "They just spit, *chtth . . . chtth.*"

I didn't want to leave Italy when the year was up and seized every opportunity I could to return. I saved up money and visited at Christmas, then the summer, then my junior year abroad, then I moved there after college thinking I would live there forever. My mother started coming back too, and after her parents died, she figured out a way to buy a small house in the Casentino, about an hour east of Florence through mountain roads. It was her summer house and my base of operations. When I moved to Italy again after 9/11, I stayed in her house. That sweet unfamiliarity wore off without me even noticing around the same time I stopped needing to disappear, and I realized somewhere along the line that I had learned Italian—not from a textbook, I just knew it. The pleasure of not belonging, however, never wore off. I was always a visitor, a foreigner. It was, I think, my fortress against being misunderstood.

On Translation's Inadequacies (In Two Languages)

Pio

Birds speak systematically. The bigger the bird, the louder the voice. The louder your voice, the more love you find. The more love you find, the more love you give. Whence love whence faith. With faith, you leap. With faith, little bird, you fly.

Birds, I learned as a young woman, speak differently in Italian. As do dogs. Dogs say "*bau bau.*" Roosters say "*circhirichu.*" And birds, chicks to be precise, say "*pio*" to mean "chirp" or "tweet." *Pio* also means pious. And Pio is a proper name—as in Padre Pio, the beloved saint who came from Puglia, a region in southern Italy.

—Cosa fa un pulcino di 40kg?
—Non so. Cosa fa un pulcino di 40 chili?
—Fa PIO PIO PIO.

Anche se gli uccellini parlano la lingua di fede, non vuol dire che è una lingua semplice. L'uomo Pio che conobbi, non lo era. Pio non fu pio. Tutt'altro. Noi ragazze lo chiamammo Il Lupo. Cose cosi: —Com'è andato con Il Lupo 'sto weekend? —Bene. Andato veloce senza freni. Freni... Non frenare. Parlavo cosi perché ero principiante e Pio me l'aveva insegnato. Ero giovane, semplice, piena di fede nel domani. Una gallina, piccola, tenera, preda di notte agli avanzi del lupo.

I knew a man from Naples named Pio—not a saint. Not even a little. We called him the Wolf. Wolves *ululano*. Pio was a wolf—all Drakkar Noir and a fussily groomed five o'clock shadow. Pio and I both worked for a small company that ran LCD subtitles at film festivals and one weekend ended up together alone in a hotel in Pescara, a battered cotton candy beach city on the eastern coast of Italy. My Italian was crummy. Although I'd lived in Italy for almost two years, I was only just beginning to have the courage to say things. I was eighteen; courage was capricious and often more reckless than it was impressive. For some reason that wasn't clear to me in the moment but became so later, Pio spent a great deal of our first meal together that weekend trying to teach me the meaning and pronunciation of the word *frenare*—to brake, like the squealing brakes of a car. It is astonishing how long perfectly bright people can discuss the meaning of words with beginning speakers and have it pass as actual conversation. Really, you don't need small talk skills if you're an American abroad. Especially if you're pretty, blond, innocent, so young you don't know the difference between reckless and courageous. Between faith and falling. Between braking and breaking.

—What does an eighty-pound chickadee say?
—I don't know. What does an eighty-pound chickadee say?
—He says, TWEET. TWEET. TWEET.

Between Translation

My mother and I argued at length about the translation of the word *alma*, which appeared in a line of poetry she was setting to music. She set poetry to music all the time, but it was often instrumental and so she didn't always use the poetry itself in the final piece. The words themselves were inspiration and incidental. But she always included the poetry in her program notes and often consulted me about the Italian translations. We disagreed about *alma*, which has several meanings in Italian but in English it's just a proper name that seems derived from "alms." In the end we agreed that all translations were inadequate but settled on the English word "sigh," because that's what the music it had inspired sounded like.

I worked once with a famous author on a translation of his short stories. People kept asking me if he was an asshole, because that was his reputation locally. I found him instead to be charming, respectful, dedicated to his art and his beautiful wife. We labored over his lush, baroque stories, stacked with literary references that spanned periods and languages, complicated by his impatient, roguish, and ambitious mind. We spent many ten-hour days comparing texts and choices, confirming variations and testing the implications of every English decision

Se c'è fosse solo un modo unico dire una cosa, non ci sarebbe bisogno degli scrittori, ovvero il bisogno ci sarebbe già stato, compiuto, tempo fa nella C'era una volta. Detto. Fatto. Non c'è da dire niente di più. Finché le cose non si cambino da se, senza l'intervento linguistico.

Invece siamo noi tutti esperti dei varianti, noi traduttori delle esperienze della vita e dalle ombre, di quello che è e quello che viene detto su quello stato. Sia meglio. Sia diverso. Io lo capisco così. Tu lo capisci cosà. E cosi vanno i verbi. Senza di che ci troviamo in compagnia di uno scrittore di discreto fama in sua casa gentile in un elegante quartiere della città, noi due, volte intense, insieme seduti davanti ad una scrivania d'autore molto ben curata, le pagine scolte dappertutto con degli appunti nelle margini in due anche tre lingue fallite. Chiedo. Ascolto. Che angoscia per lo scrittore, che fatica l'essere preciso ed evocativo. Lunga pausa e lo scrittore e la moglie ballano una bellissima danza stile Portoghese. Il consumato non ha traduzione. E se non questo . . . Che angoscia l'essere imprigionato dall'idea che ci sia solamente un verbo. Ed è verbo suo. E se ho capito bene, vorrei sapere che cose succeda quando muore?

I made. We'd break for strong sweet black coffee, and one day instead of coffee he and his wife danced. They twirled gorgeously and easily around the living room—as if the word "intricacy" had never been invented. Piteous fado on the record player turned up to a deafening volume.

All translations are inadequate and just before the book was sent to press he fired me.

I stopped translating. And more recently he died. There is no trace of the stories I wrote from his stories. My version is gone and so there is one less reading in the world of his immutable words.

Alma che fai?

Something I always resented about Italy (at least the Italy I lived in as a young woman) was that if two couples went out, the men would sit together in the front of the car and the women in the back. God forbid a woman drive when a man's available to do it better. No chance at all that you'd want to spend any part of the double date talking to your boyfriend. Less chance even that you'd want to spend it talking to your friend's boyfriend. Obviously, if it was just the two of you alone, you always got to ride up front, and routinely as if he were engaging a parking brake, your boyfriend would stick one

Da una lingua ad un'altra cambia il cervello, dai ritmi, sensi, colorature. Questo è il perché alma può significare anima spirito nutrice sospiro in Italiano ed in Inglese no. Alma era una parola che discutevo molto con mia mamma prima che morì. "Spirito" dissi. "Sospiro" disse. Ma in verità lei non doveva mai scegliere perché lei si esprimeva in lingua musicale. Spesso componeva musica ad una poesia italiana senza neanche usare le parole della poesia nella musica. La parola ispira la musica. Un passo oltre traduzione andava la mamma, un passo che esprima tutti i valori di una parola. Eppure io, andando un passo hand between your legs and drive, oltre in un'altra direzione faccio shift, and smoke with the other. conto ora che parlare italiano, Because Italy is like that (at least the scrivere italiano, pensare italiano, è quello che facevo da Italy I lived in). One night we were ragazza. Ed ora non la sono più. out with Fulvio, who was an actor, Se traduco da italiano attraverso and his date, who was English. Her non solamente la lingua ma name might have been Rose or Alma. anche un tempo. Se parlo Either name works because we only italiano mi esprimo nella voce di ever met her that one time—like so una ragazza, con pensieri, spiriti, many of Fulvio's passions. Rose and sospiri da ragazza. Giovane io I gossiped together in the backseat sono in italiano. Sciocca pure. because that was the friendly thing E beh. Per lo meno sto qui, a visitare un po' con la mamma.

to do, and Fulvio, the actor, who had briefly and uncharacteristically stopped talking, suddenly remarked that I spoke entirely differently in English. He insisted that based on the few moments of conversation that he'd overheard from the backseat, I was an entirely different person in English. I volunteered that I might be smarter in English, though maybe less precise, and he said he thought instead that I was heavier somehow, more intense and a little scary. Not at all like a screeching cat. Because otherwise American girls, the way they talked, were all screeching cats.

I often thought I was happier in Italian, because somehow there was less riding on it. I didn't have to commit. At eighteen, nineteen, twenty years old, Italian was a costume I'd hide in for months at a time, smart-assed and awkward, full of wonderful sounds that I disgorged as if they were the most sophisticated primal scream therapy. When I was hiding in my Italian costume, English was transformed into a private refuge, the language of silent thoughts, puzzles of abstractions I never needed to solve because there would never be a need to express them. I said "Ti amo" to a man long before I could bring myself to say "I love you."

I was even able to say why I loved him in Italian; "*È l'unica cosa nella mia vita che capisco,*" I said—*It's the only thing in my life I'm sure of.*

THERE ARE PICTURES in my mother's photo album from when she was a young woman studying composition in Florence in the late 1950s, black-and-white photos of her and a beautiful young man on a bench in the Boboli Gardens. His short dark hair is putty thick and unruly; his big almond eyes cut back like knives along languorous cheekbones. My mother is glamorous, perfectly turned out in a trim little suit dress and patent leather pumps, her freckles standing out exotically against her pale skin, one eyebrow cocked ironically, her curly dark hair sleepily crooked as if she's just woken up from a nap on a flower bed. My mother's Fulbright grant went far in postwar Italy; she felt rich for the first time in her life. She had clothes made to order and said sometimes she'd have four stuffed artichokes for lunch, just because she wanted to. For many years, I thought the man in the picture was a boyfriend she called Claudio, who she said was always cross at her for being late.

Everything untranslatable belongs to her. Both young women in Italy, both shedding oppressive American selves, running a little, and flying a lot—we trespassed the same foreign refuge together decades apart. After she died, I sat for hours looking at those photographs, trying to conjure and consume the brilliant years of my mother's youth by the sheer effort of staring. And I suddenly saw for the first time the wedding ring on the hand draped around my mother's shoulder and realized it wasn't Claudio in the picture at all.

Author of Her Destiny

> *When people say that nothing happens in their lives, I*
> *believe them. But you must understand that everything*
> *happens to an artist; time is always redeemed, nothing*
> *is lost and wonders never cease.*
>
> —Muriel Spark, *Loitering with Intent*

There was a period in my life when the only thing I could write about was my divorce. Unfortunately, it coincided with a blossoming period in my book-reviewing career. After a decade of begging, I'd finally hit a sweet spot and editors were approaching me, instead of vice versa, to write about books. But because of my seething muted trauma, I bombed every opportunity that came my way. I became obsessive about whatever minute detail in the book seemed to relate to divorce, regret, pain, and/or loss. And if I couldn't find something that had even the slenderest tangential connection to divorce, I didn't know what to say. Dana Spiotta's National Book Award–nominated 2006 novel *Eat the Document* was "awesome." That was the substance of the five-word review I delivered. The magazine editor wrote back begging for "details." I drew a blank and the piece was killed.

There were several similar disasters before at last an astute editor said to me—after I'd turned in a twenty-three-page essay on emotional realism and divorce in the recent work of Hanif Kureishi instead of a two-page review of his new novel—"You've obviously got something that you need to get out and write about that's interfering with everything else. Come back when you've worked it out."

I alternated between divorce and writer's block for almost two years, at which point the boredom was suffocating. And so I bribed my way into an assignment to interview the writer Gary Shteyngart, which—like most interviews with Gary Shteyngart—took place in a downtown Manhattan Irish bar over sliders and tangy boutique beer. I completely forgot and didn't record or write down most of what was said (except for his recommendation to read *War and Peace* but to skip the *Peace*). Something about the warm beer and having to retrieve and invent the interview the next day catapulted me back into form. I wrote about Sontag soon after and then Gerard Manley Hopkins, and somewhere in there, I started to feel a little bit more like me again.

Then I recklessly volunteered to deliver a talk at the university where I teach about my "favorite, formative" book, *Loitering with Intent* by Muriel Spark. Six hours before the talk was scheduled to begin, I was furious, staring down an empty page and reckoning. Muriel Spark. Muriel Spark seduced me with sherry-laced tea and stinky cheese and walked me to the precipice and then hurled me down. I'd planned to give a lecture about fictional autobiography and humor: the theme, which I'd chosen intuitively and carelessly, was a minefield.

Not that there's anything wrong with humor—humor is wonderful, though ridiculously hard to pull off. Autobiography, however, *that* was my albatross. It all connected in Muriel Spark. I'd read Muriel Spark for the first time during a golden glittering period in my career and my marriage. Spark was an author my now ex-husband and I had read together. With the clock ticking down to the moment I was due to deliver myself before a crowd of sleepy MFA students, I realized that I couldn't write about my own

personal experience of Muriel Spark books without also returning
to the sinkhole of divorce and loss. And to a certain extent—in
honor of Ms. Spark and her fully tragic heroes—self-immolation.

BACK TO MY mother's house in Italy, to that strangely romantic
antediluvian time: my then-boyfriend and I were living in that
teetering stone house in the densely forested hills of eastern
Tuscany, not far in fact from where Dame Muriel Spark (and her
faithful companion Penelope Jardine) lived out the last decades of
her life. The mountain winters made your bones cold and the old
stone houses, tucked into that extraordinary landscape thick with
ancient trees glistening green with morning and afternoon dew,
were damp. It made Dame Muriel's back ache. It made everything I
owned, clothing, books, shampoo, smell permanently of must.

My boyfriend and I were both working on books. This was my
exploration of the history of religious calling combined with a family
memoir. I had no idea what I was doing, but it involved reading
Thomas Merton and Norman Mailer, and complaining about my
mother. I was also working on a translation for the publishing company New Directions, which was a childhood dream realized. I'd set
my sights on New Directions long before I moved to New York. (In
fact, I confused New Directions with New York. There was a time I
thought New York City was a cigarette-smoke-laced office on Four-
teenth Street and Eighth Avenue where Tennessee Williams drolly
worked reception, Lawrence Ferlinghetti served coffee and sang
fado, and Ezra Pound was kept locked in the supply closet.)

Due to my unreconstructed love for New Directions, we
had developed a friendship with an editor there, Barbara Epler, a
disheveled waspy beauty with a riding-school ponytail and wanton
lipstick. Barbara had started at New Directions the summer she
graduated from Harvard and has never worked anywhere else.

Today she is the editor in chief. She was charming and intellectual and drank bourbon straight up. I told her she was pretty the first time I met her, while I was interviewing her for a magazine article. Something about her seemed to demand awkward candor. Her German companion, Claudia, made me think of peaches and fishnet stockings. She was like a lovely unmarred refugee from a Nathanael West novel. She flirted as she breathed.

Barbara and Claudia were planning a European tour and were going to spend a weekend with us in Italy on their way to visit Muriel Spark. For months before their arrival, Barbara had been plying us by mail with the Spark novels that New Directions was in the process of reissuing: *Memento Mori, The Girls of Slender Means, The Ballad of Peckham Rye, Loitering with Intent*. We devoured each book as it arrived. The copy of *Loitering with Intent* I'm holding has my penciled notes in it under my now ex-husband's penned notes, his precise miniature dog ears marking so very many pages that the book is bloated to three times its original volume. If you were to ask me to pick some juicy quotes from the book, I'd merrily copy out the entire book. Have you ever had a book like that?

Barbara tried to help my husband set up an interview with Spark for the *Paris Review* Writers at Work series in advance of the visit—we were not-so-secretly desperate to actually meet her in the flesh and an interview was an unimpeachable excuse. After many frustrated attempts at diplomacy, much faxing, and wheedling, the interview never came to pass. Muriel Spark didn't trust *The Paris Review*. An interview had once been attempted; it had been a disaster with lots of impolitic missteps and she refused to risk a repeat situation. She was a complicated woman.

But we found other ways to invoke Muriel Spark. My husband wrote about *Loitering with Intent* as an antidote to Ian McEwan's *Atonement*, which he'd already reviewed negatively but hated so dearly that he needed to revile it a second time. Meanwhile I was mostly using her to rest my eyes from the dense religious matter I was reading during the day—Kierkegaard and John Henry Newman (who figures largely in *Loitering with Intent*). I scoured Spark's "memoir" *Curriculum Vitae* for her conversion story (I was collecting them for my book; hers, to Catholicism, then to some obscure self-loathing Judaism that alienated her from her own son, seemed juicy) but I came up empty. In addition to being a complicated woman, she was a cagey memoirist, omitting and even outright lying when it suited her.

Before you grow too cross with her for withholding, you must remember that she was, above all else, a novelist. Her memoir is frustrating, but her novel—her *autobiographical* novel—*Loitering with Intent* is "clear crystal" (as she might say). Nothing could be a clearer crystal indictment of the art of memoir than *Loitering with Intent*, the story of a struggling young poet, Fleur Talbot, who lands herself a job as secretary to the Autobiographical Association. The Association is a group of elderly people, "men and women of great distinction living fully, very full, lives," who are, alas, "largely unaccustomed to literary composition." They meet once a week to read and critique each other's memoirs, which will ultimately be deposited in a vault for seventy years, "until all the living people mentioned therein shall be living no longer."

I REALIZED, AS I sat in front of the blank sheet of paper that was supposed to be my lecture, locking Muriel Spark more and more firmly into this one particular moment of my past life, the old lady had a message for me.

What in the world can anyone know about the depths of your heart? Muriel Spark didn't want to be depicted and, after years of cooperating with the writer Martin Stannard, she concluded that he was betraying her and stripped him of his status as her authorized biographer. He'd misrepresented, or perhaps simply misunderstood, her. Spark was a difficult person. The *New Yorker* editor Ved Mehta famously said of her that she "went through people like pieces of Kleenex." She was also, in Stannard's depiction, "hypersensitive to insult." It is said that she broke entirely with her book editor, Peter Mayer, when he allowed a paperback edition of her book *The Comforters* to be issued with cover copy that read: "a witty and mysterious prank." Spark would have phrased it differently.

Spark wasn't a prankster but she was a wit. And she wasn't a memoirist but she was a novelist. Sometimes she was an autobiographical novelist, who mined the often cruel and squalid circumstances of her life for astute and somewhat wicked allegories. What a wonderful charm, I think now, to be able to weave stories out of—and over—an unforgiving life.

OUR TUSCAN IDYLL was more than fifteen years ago. At seven, our son has difficulty comprehending that my ex-husband and I were ever married, let alone in love. "Have you ever met my grandpa?" he asks me quite reasonably. "Of course," I say—without actually explaining that his grandfather had been my father-in-law and used to read every review I wrote and immediately e-mail me long, thoughtful comments.

One day, sitting in front of the computer together, studying a Weather Channel video stream of lightning flashes as seen from outer space, I said without thinking, "Your father used to be obsessed with tracking tropical storms on the Internet too!" He looked at me blankly. "It's genetic," I tried to explain. "And box scores. He was always checking box scores." His father and I living together, being a couple, was an abstraction to him. He was wondering why something he did made me think of his father.

He can't remember the time before he was born to the exact same extent you can't remember something that happened to me in another country, fifteen years ago. All anyone (including my son) gets are the stories that I choose to tell, or not; that I choose to cast as triumphs, comedies, or the God's honest truth. Last summer, I randomly started telling him a funny story about how angry his father got at me for hiccupping too loudly one parched afternoon at the ruins of Villa Jovis on the island of Capri. The two of us were alone among the ancient rocks, having set out for a mad-dog high-noon hike, like the American tourists we were. We were heading up a sandy path to the highest point of Tiberius's former palace, where it is said by some he debauched women and then threw them off the cliff. Use and toss. My hiccups were echoing and, it seemed, loud enough to rouse the ghosts. I couldn't keep quiet enough to match the solemnity or beauty of the rocky crest.

"No, Mommy," my son corrected me. "You accidentally said you were with Daddy."

This is how the past gets reverse engineered. But you don't actually want to rewrite it, you just want to recolor it, make it witty and heroic. And yet not so much so that your son can't recognize that it's you in the story.

I WAS NEVER good at making stuff up; I'm much more interested in parsing the density, inanity, confusion, and occasional brilliance of life around me. Doing constant battle with the sense that I can't, and won't, be able to include everything. But if I *could* invent rather than just observe, I would. Because fiction writers have so very much more access to truth—some kind of truth, at least. Even truths draped in delusion or hope, a world gone so mad it couldn't possibly resemble reality—even those upside-down, backward truths speak volumes about what's missing, what's desired, about the world the way we wish it were.

Spark explicitly described *Loitering with Intent* as an "autobiographical novel." Here are some of the facts it draws on: It is set during the period when in real life Spark was twenty-nine years old and had just taken over the editorship of *The Poetry Review*, a fusty literary publication lorded over by reactionary metronome poets. Spark had vowed to rejuvenate it but instead got embroiled in a nasty political battle with the board and a number of elderly men who wanted to have an affair with her but not be edited by her. Several other married or elderly men with whom she became seriously involved eventually complicated her station at the review beyond repair, and she was cast out. She was poor, addicted to diet pills, and just wanted to write.

Novelized: The hero of *Loitering with Intent* is a twenty-nine-year-old poet, having just taken on this position at the Autobiographical Association, is embroiled in a doomed love affair, and is pillaging everyone and everything around her for material for her own novel in progress, *Warrender Chase*. Ultimately her charges at the Autobiographical Association discover that she is betraying them—depicting them without their permission or oversight. She is fired but the book she wrote is a success. In other words, Muriel Spark's great autobiographical novel was *all about* writing about and being written about. It is about the massive swaths of fiction embroidered over real life, the impossibility of a true portrait or self-portrait, and about how funny we all get, and how funny we all are, about being misunderstood. Because truthfully, being misunderstood is a searing pain. And there was a lot to misunderstand about Muriel Spark.

Spark's de-authorized biographer comes to the excellent conclusion that Spark's self-portrait as Fleur Talbot excises all the anxiety and unhappiness of the real period in Muriel's life and that her autobiographical vision exists in the privileged dimension of a purely creative life. Missing from her fictional autobiography: drug addiction, doomed romances, domestic abuse, and total abject failure as a mother. "*Loitering*," wrote Stannard, "transforms the narrative of her own tortured life during these years into one celebrating triumph over adversity, self-belief justified."

Loitering is about becoming a writer. The self-assured, intelligent, and snarky young writer in these pages is positively heroic. But she isn't a real twenty-nine-year-old (which is how old I was when I read it for the first time); she's a sixty-year-old woman in disguise, a woman who can look back and know for sure what matters and what's going to stick, and build her hero from there. Difficult, disappointing people are preposterous and hilarious, reduced merely to some "hundreds of words." It's aspirational past tense; total control; a way of redrawing the past so that regret is rewritten as conviction.

"I HAVE A strong sense that fiction is lies," Spark once said. But she could lie more truthfully in her autobiographical novel than she could in her memoir, which was full of lies of omission (and not much else). It was the vindication of revisionist history, I might have said in the lecture that I delivered the morning after—a literary lesson punctuated with confessions and unexpected intimacies.

There is in fact some too-dreary quality to autobiography, a slavish obligation to control the slippery world of memories, to reckon and to justify. What I admire so deeply about Dame Muriel is that she embraces the lies and then, deploying her punctuation and sentences and paragraphs, extricates herself. And she does it with joyful aplomb, disguising, maybe even defying, the wreckage of real life. Life is bigger than just one story, hope is a powerful instinct, heroes rise again from the fiery embers, and ultimately, it's much nicer to laugh about what's lost than it is to cry.

On Fate and Facts

Our fate spends itself in this succession of hopes and regrets.
—Natalia Ginzburg, "Winter in the Abruzzi"

One afternoon, I was driving my children to gymnastics class in Bay Ridge, Brooklyn, and bumbling with considerable difficulty through an explanation of the difference between pop and classical music. With the White Stripes hammering irresistibly in the background, I couldn't for the life of me think of something useful to say—"That drum beat, there. You know it's coming, and that makes you happy. In classical music you wouldn't know there was a drum beat there . . ."

The song clanged to a perfect resolution and the iPod shuffled right on to the first haunting twangs of a Dolly Parton song. A roar of protest rose up from the backseat: "Mommy! This is a slow song! We don't like slow songs!"

The mood in the car turned suddenly so anti-intellectual I felt defiant. "No," I corrected. "This is a sad song. It's entirely different." The music swelled and Dolly's voice tumbled, *And then I felt the lonely—coming down.* "You don't even have to understand the words," I said. "You can hear from the music that it's sad." I had a keen memory of my own mother trying to teach me that even when Tristan and Isolde thought they were mortal enemies, they were lovers.

"The words are irrelevant," she told me. "It doesn't matter what they think they're saying; they're singing a love song."

"Mommy!" my daughter, four at the time, persisted. "We don't like sad songs!"

"No, Anna," said Isaac. "Actually, I do like sad songs. I want to hear this."

And in the rearview mirror I could see him turning his serious little face away from his sister to look out the window, his brow knit in concentration as he tried to hear in the music what I was saying. I realized that unlike my mother, who actually knew music theory and could have demonstrated the specific tonal progression that proved the love song buried in that first *Tristan and Isolde* duet, I was shooting wildly with my lesson. But at least I had sabotaged the rash rejection, the automatic response, and Isaac was trying to understand something (anything) new. The road curved out farther to the west and the sun broke over the Verrazano, flooding the car with light.

I AM NOT a gatherer of facts—I prefer to work from a gestural understanding of matter. It's a kind of disability. And yet, information today cooperates. It is voluble, filtered, impressionistic, and subordinate to a vast spectrum of unquantifiables: Why does the burping kitten video go viral? Why does that family have a four-story town house on the park? Why does this family have a predisposition to suicide? How big does the print on a map need to be in order to cause the least frustration across the thirty-to-seventy-five-year-old demographic? When to deploy the

destructive impulse hard-wired in every single human being—
young, old, brilliant, disabled? Murder, hunting, divorce, beheading
dolls. Is there good destruction? Who is setting that meter? And
why can't you reprogram a cat to scratch somewhere besides the
arm of the couch? Who programmed the cat to scratch there in
the first place? Why can you reprogram a dog? God is in our DNA.
Happiness is chemistry. Happiness is circumstantial.

THE SCHOOL PARENT coordinator, who behind the librarian
hairdo and heavy-framed glasses looks like she might have started
out as Miss Subways 1976, frequently greets us in the school lobby
in the mornings with a bullhorn, urging us to *leave* our children
in the lobby and *move* quickly out of the way, for "there are many
parents trying to drop off *their* children too. Parents, say your good-
byes, please, and move on."

Most of us can't hear her, even through the bullhorn, over the
din of 850 children. The ones who do roll their eyes, because school
was different when we were children and it was right then and
somehow perverted now. We walked to second grade, and walked
home again. We were never *escorted* to our classrooms. We didn't
have city police working the sign-in desk at the entrance. We had
the old man at Anderson Jewelers—probably Anderson himself—
who stood on the front step of the store reading the newspaper
until 8:30, when the school bell rang, at which point he rolled up
his paper and swatted any children rounding the corner to the
school—and there was no alternative direct route to school—
on the butt. I was terrified of the old man, the shame of getting
swatted right there in the middle of the town's main intersection.
But the fear didn't get me out the door quicker in the morning, it
just made me panic, fall to my knees, and sob and beg my mother to
drive me when I was late—which was most mornings.

On the mornings when, for some unholy reason, I had enough time to walk to school unmolested, I'd cut down Denton Road and through the opening in the hedge at the bottom of the U-turn and walk along the Brook Path, coming in through the back of the building and avoiding the town center entirely. Until Leslie Danovitch told me there was a boogeyman who lived on the Brook Path and he ate little children. I never walked that way again, choosing the fear and shame of Old Man Anderson over the nightmare of being attacked and "eaten," even after my father explained to me that there was no such thing as a boogeyman, which I've conflated in my mind with the time he told me what sexual intercourse was, adding that the appalling feat he described actually "sort of felt good."

These conversations with my father, in my absurd memory, took place in the cramped hallway on the second floor of our house, right at the point where the hall took a sudden, useless turn, a place where no one in their right mind would hold any conversation. And in this memory, where my father is describing sex in the hallway right outside the door to my mother's room, the door is open just enough so that I can see the bed, which my mother is on, though she was never on her bed in the middle of the day except when she was dying on it thirty years later—an image that seared itself so deeply into my mind's eye that I can't see that bed in any memory at all without her lying on it, dying.

And although my father was correct about sex, he was wrong about the boogeyman, because just two years later an eight-year-old girl from my new school in Ohio was abducted on her way home from detention and not eaten but raped and bludgeoned. My strongest memory after that is of a mimeographed sign taped to lampposts with a dark sketch of a man with black hair and a blunt nose under the words "HAVE YOU SEEN THIS MAN?"

Someone did, in fact, see him—had seen in fact the very moment of her getting taken, witnessed the interaction, not knowing until later, of course, what it was that he had seen. He saw enough to give a description to a police sketch artist. Will he ever—if he even was a he, even was an adult—I wonder, ever stop seeing that man? I can't remember that poor girl's face because my absurd memory has superimposed it over the police sketch so that I think she was a dark girl, with black hair, and a blunt nose.

That was also the same year my parents got divorced. My most distinct memory is of them standing outside by the car having the conversation in which they decided they were getting divorced and me and my sister running around and around the house, whizzing by them and making a lot of noise, trying futilely to get their attention. From that isolated year we lived in Ohio as a family before returning, defeated—my mother, sister, and I—to Boston, I remember only that conversation and the incident with the bubble-gum-flavored ice cream from which I was able to retrieve seventeen gumballs—all of which I put in my mouth at once. Being frozen made the gum slimy and chunky. I blew a formidable bubble with that horrid viscous mass, but since I was in the backseat of the car and the window was open, the wind flew in and whipped the bubble right into my long hair and the gum didn't come out even when my mother tried to pick it out using peanut butter to loosen it and so we had to cut it. Nothing was ever the same.

THE EMERGENCY FORM I signed on the kids' first day of school asked whether there was anyone who *wasn't* allowed to pick up your children. And then the follow-up question: Is there a court-ordered restraining order in place protecting your child? And, I wonder, if there were a restraining order, how would they enforce it? With a bullhorn? We parents are corralled each morning and evening and encouraged to keep moving, to not block the entryways, to find our children, to leave our children, and move along. I signed another permission slip, acknowledging that I'd been alerted that our public school was participating in a beta version of the Lockdown Drill, a school shooting preparedness measure that's being instituted across the country during which the children learn to hide and keep silent while the principal or police guard walks down the hall banging on doors and yelling. The idea makes my stomach turn, and it's only natural to assume that it would lead the children to be frightened of a psycho with an automatic weapon. But my son reports that it makes him feel safe, that he would know what to do if a bad guy got into the school. I grew up convinced that we would be obliterated by a nuclear bomb. Having grown up with that specter, I suppose the idea of a psycho with a gun is less terrifying. Although, during our nuclear attack drills, we didn't have the same kind of responsibility that my children bear—to be quiet, to hide well. In our drills, we just had to get under our desks, which we all knew wasn't going to keep us safe from anything. Lack of responsibility, lack of agency. No one ever told me that if I was a good girl and kept very quiet, Russia wouldn't bomb Boston. What I did know was that if it happened—especially living as we did in the technology corridor off Route 128, a first-strike target—we would be dust and so would our parents. Perhaps there is a mercy in total instant obliteration that I could appreciate even as a child, whereas a school shooting has no such mercy. But my children don't have the nuclear option as a point of comparison.

Too much time travel. I have a nosebleed.

BECAUSE OUT OF the whirl, what I know, what I don't know, and how to organize the chaos around me, there's a small reedy voice deep in the background, surprisingly audible over the din. It's not fair, repeats the voice. There's nothing for it. But it's not fair, she says.

But I also remember the blizzard of 1977, when the schools were closed for a week and Governor Dukakis postponed Valentine's Day so that the kids wouldn't have to miss it. Time was in constant motion when I was young. Now time is white noise, rushing and paralyzing; time is everything that's unfixable.

THERE ARE TWO distinct, but not dissociable, kinds of memory: autobiographical and semantic. Each kind triggers different regions of the brain, which is why neurobiologists are able to map how we remember what. Semantic memories are essentially random, word- and fact-driven. I assume that semantic memories provide the spelling for "February," the date upon which Napoleon was assassinated, the rote recitation "Shall I compare thee to a summer's day?" Autobiographical memory is episodic and relies on how an event made you feel. Autobiographical memory is specifically narrative, which, I assume, often leaves it open to terrific sins of embellishment, omission, and suggestion—but these same qualities also make the memories endure.

The 1980 rape and murder in Upper Arlington of eight-year-old Asenath Dukat, my schoolmate, brought horror and fear with it. I was surprised, looking back over newspaper clippings, to find that I had remembered the tragedy with uncharacteristic clarity. I have always tended to overdramatization, so I set about fact-checking my fourth-grade memory with the assumption that I had made large parts of it up. But, except for the wool watch cap I'd included on the suspect in my mental image of the police artist sketch, I had remembered it the way it had happened.

Historians make abstract facts into narratives, imbuing events with cause and effect, ideally building an emotional component into what could also be seen as a random string of events. It is a storytelling technique that evolved from how our brains are wired to remember things. We remember where we put the Drano because we can imagine a story about what would happen if we left it out and a child got ahold of it. We don't remember random strings of numbers, but we do memorize phone numbers of people. I was taught, but don't remember how, to multiply fractions. I remember the day my parents decided to divorce, because that day, running around the car wasn't an isolated fact in time, but rather the first memory in a series of memories that I felt deeply.

We *had* to invent History because it's intrinsic to our thought patterns. Yesterday is a story as much as Napoleon is a story as much as the story we imagine about what would happen with the Drano. And that's where it gets really interesting: our imagination is a component of our memory, and the stronger our imagination, the stronger our capacity for memory. There is a related correlation to our ability to imagine a future. A richly imagined future is entirely dependent on our ability to remember the past. Likewise the structure of our memories—whether we're people with stronger semantic or autobiographical memories—will influence the structure of what we imagine and how we conceive of the future.

Memory is an entire field of neurological science. Of course it is. This is how a group of memory experts at Harvard University explains it:

> *One of the most fascinating aspects of human cognition is our ability to withdraw from the current moment and to mentally transport ourselves to another time, place, or perspective.*

> *Collectively, the abilities to remember the past via episodic auto-*
> *biographical memory, or to imagine possible future events, rep-*
> *resent important expressions of the human memory system,*
> *potentially conferring a significant adaptive advantage in plan-*
> *ning for the future.*

I remember minutely how I imagined my future self as a young girl. In my future, I would have smooth hair and dress like Lauren Bacall. I would live in a house with marble floors, high ceilings, a tiled kitchen, oversized windows, and a living room furnished with modular Italian furniture in primary colors that was so well made that it would look fabulous even if children made forts out of it. Aside from the purely fantastical elements that involved me being a pristine housekeeper and tall, the rest of this imaginary future of mine is patently a vision of order and wealth. And now I live in the future, and it is nothing like what I imagined.

But I remember what I imagined, and in hindsight can recognize that fantasy for what it is: a mirror image, reversed in every respect, of the childhood I remember. The stories that stand out: the almost stepped on a rattlesnake story; the driving through Memphis the night Elvis died to visit my great cousin Flora story; the crazy relative from Georgia who looked like Sissy Spacek and lived with us for a while before moving to New York to become a Mooney; how she used to bring me with her to the bar on Route 9 and ply me with Shirley Temples until she finished her shift; the night I startled her while sleepwalking and she screamed and screamed because she thought I was a ghost; the time we had to take our long drive from Massachusetts to my dad's house for Christmas vacation through the Poconos instead of via Interstate 80, so that Daddy could take advantage of downhill momentum to coast so that the gas would last us to Ohio.

•

AFTER DROPPING THE kids off, instead of preparing to teach my class, I've been dwelling in my memories and now I'm the one who will be late for school. As I walk across campus toward my classroom, "Free Bird" blasting in my headphones, my brain is a big static. I am completely unprepared to teach. It is as if someone took me offline. Five months into the semester, my students look unfamiliar, with rosy faces, round unblinking eyes, and shiny bulb bodies. Someone sent in the doll replacements today. And if you were to approach me, touch me on the shoulder to soothe me, your hand would pass right through me into air, because somewhere between getting out of bed this morning and *Won't you fly high, free bird?* I've become a hologram. *Lord knows, I can't change.*

It may all work out, nonetheless. I know the piece I am teaching today very well, a short essay by the Italian writer Natalia Ginzburg. I've read it, written about it, even translated it from Italian so that I could be sure I was precisely understanding its mechanics. It is "Winter in the Abruzzi," about the few years that Ginzburg and her family spent in political exile in southern Italy, a sublime illustration of how memory punishes.

The essay starts with the bleak description of an isolated landscape where there are only two seasons, summer and winter—and summer is over by the third sentence. It is a remote place, rural, cut off from education, culture, and the political activities of northern Italy. The villagers are simple and missing teeth; they revere the Ginzburg family, those northerners, for their education and criticize them for their bizarre modern habits: *Taking walks in winter?* Over the course of their exile, the village becomes more familiar and the family's homesickness endures. They spend much of their time in Abruzzo writing home for news, missing friends and family, and looking forward to it all being over. Shortly after they do return, Ginzburg's husband, Leone, is arrested, tortured, and executed. And Ginzburg ends the essay by saying that the unendurable exile was the best time of her life. She squandered it wishing for it to end, and she's spent the many years since then wishing she could go back and appreciate that time: *Era quello il tempo migliore della mia vita a solo adesso che m'è sfuggito per sempre solo adesso lo so . . .* Those were the best years of my life, and I only know it now that they're gone forever.

"Our dreams," she writes, "are never realized and as soon as we see them destroyed we realize that the most intense joys of our lives aren't part of its reality. As soon as we see them destroyed, we're consumed with nostalgia for that time when those dreams burned yet brightly."

This is what I know. Anxiety—about teaching, about money, about school shootings—is not a story. Because that is not what matters. And everything that does matter, that does endure, is subjected to the perversions of memory anyway, and its mutters and clutters and scars, all context and sad songs but no comprehension.

A Mystic at Heart

"If your mother had brought you for a reading the day you were born," said the Astrologer, "I would have said: Mom, tell this kid that when she gets to '07, she's going to enter into a very nutty time. And nothing in her life is going to go according to schedule, and it's not of her own doing. If before '07, she settles down in the suburbs and has two-point-five kids and an SUV and one-point-two dogs and a white picket fence and all that stuff, she's just going to end up walking out on her family, saying 'I've had it.'"

So, this was destined to be a period of destruction, dismantling, and derangement in my life. There were too many stars vying for predominance. I couldn't be true to any of them; I couldn't be partial to some of them. They all had contradicting imperatives: take heed of your mortality, live large, lighten up, get serious, fall in love, date a lot, get married, have kids, travel, laugh, cry, feel shame, stop living for other people, buy shoes, be thrifty, go barefoot, cut the cord, hang tight. Or, as the Astrologer put it, "You're in a crucible of chaos."

My Brooklyn neighborhood was kind of like a suburb. I didn't have the white picket fence and two-point-five kids, but I did have a new marriage to a man I'd been with for a long time and loved entirely, I'd recently published a book, I was in excellent health, I was on boards of charitable organizations and a Jewish group, the house was tidy and attractive, our cat was a stunner, my family was proud of me, I was proud of me. And then I did just pick up and leave. And I had a baby. And my mother died. Everything that I didn't know about life converged on this astonishing moment. It's Pluto's fault. He kills everything so that it can be reborn.

I AM A skeptic. The Astrologer confirmed it: "In youth, your chart is that of the disbeliever," he said, "the one who doesn't want to give over, the one who asks a lot of questions, too many questions."

Or I *was* a skeptic. "The older you get," he continued, "the more this turns into the chart of the mystic." I was a communist at four; a sharp-tongued atheist by fifteen; at twenty-five, I was, like my mother, occasionally curious about but essentially uninterested in Judaism except with regard to the Holocaust. I was also at this time transitioning out of a collegiate aversion to identity politics and into an incipient sentimental yearning for "family" (though I didn't know yet exactly what I meant by that). When I turned thirty, my father, whom I worshipped but who always lived too far away, told me he wanted to become an Episcopal priest. The depth of his spiritual life and religious convictions came as an embarrassing surprise to me—a demonstration of how partially I was involved in his vast second life, and my first intimate encounter with the unique and private nature of religious experience. Shamefully, I understood nothing about his spirit or religion, or how it fit into our tenuously shared adult life. I wrote a book about it—about faith, the language of faith, what it meant to him, what it did and didn't mean to me as I understood it, what I inherited of his lapsed and regained Christianity, how very much I shared of my mother's secular and sporadically spiritual Judaism. For me, the whole subject was essentially unexplored intellectual territory: philosophy with consequence and conviction, philosophy with ambition.

My book editor kept describing the project as a quest. I kept resisting that description; it seemed too syndicated-UHF-television for me. I wasn't struggling with a quest as much as I was reveling in a burgeoning impression of what having answers might feel like. The religious discussions I had while researching my book began to provide a kind of clearinghouse for all of my basic adult concerns: Why did I believe in marriage even after my parents had made such a mash of theirs? Why did I prize family even though mine was only partially functional? What purpose the life of the mind? And so on.

The Judaism of my demographic—the Judaism I found while working on my book—was wildly appealing. It seduced the sentimental skeptic in me: community-driven, well-oiled, white-collar, and doggedly intellectual. Praying stood in for studying, hard questions had answers in textual riddles, and the moral structure seemed earthy and practical. It was a world of listservs and boisterous children, and well-appointed homes stuffed with books, wine, and (sometimes) salami. It was hard not to love it, hard not to feel secure in that world, to feel as if you were going to be okay, no matter how anarchic your past, how insecure your professional world, how deeply ingrained your patterns of confusion, how manipulative your mother, or how mortal.

This was, in no small sense, a palpable model of everything I hoped for from my life. I never wanted a big bling ring or a white princess dress, I just desperately wanted an intact family. The Jews had a strategy: honor the mind, cherish your family, do good in the world. It was almost like a science of hope.

And then everything collapsed. I was thirty-five and all of my new faith shook, twisted, and then evaporated—as if it had never been there at all. After a fifteen-year battle, my mother's breast cancer metastasized to her skin and collarbone. My fiancé had sex with someone else, and so we got married. He took a job in another state I didn't want to go to. I had an affair with a married man, and he left his wife and I left my husband. In the midst of that nightmare, I got pregnant, had a baby. My mother died. The bricks and mortar of my dream fell away. I cried for a year. I felt like I was losing my mind. As far as doing good—I might as well have lashed a bayonet to my forehead. All that high-minded Jewishness puckered and curled back from the surface, a shiny, heat-resistant veneer.

"So," THE ASTROLOGER said, "the first God competing for your attention is Saturn. Saturn is all about mortality. He's the responsible one, the mature one. He's the stern voice of your conscience; he's about shame and guilt. He's saying, 'Get your act together . . . Get married, have children.'"

My husband and I had been engaged for a year and were regularly attending a Judaism 101 for Adults class when we first approached the rabbi about getting married with a Jewish ceremony. I was an eager but unlearned Jew; he was an open-minded atheist. The rabbi didn't always perform mixed marriages but made an exception for us. We promised to raise our eventual children Jewish (as opposed to with no religion).

We agreed on a lot of things (meatballs, Naples, the importance of hills), but I think our mutual desire for stability came to settle on a hyperfunctional brand of Judaism—frank, routine, urban. It was Norman Rockwell compared with how we'd been brought up. There was something charming and optimistic about having God at the center. It gave us confidence in our future.

When my fiancé told me he'd had sex with someone else—a revelation that came on the heels of the news that my mother had run out of treatment options—he said, "I've ruined our life." I rushed to reassure him. I believed that the life we'd built was too strong to be ruined. I guess I'd also believed that he would never do that to me.

There was the most peculiar moment, soon after that, when we went to the rabbi's house to talk about the wedding. Sitting with the rabbi in his living room, chatting about family, instructional books to read, useful Judaica to acquire, and dates—my husband said that he thought he might want to convert. Despite all the studying and signing on to a Jewish wedding and children, I hadn't ever considered the possibility of a full conversion. I responded with amazement, "But you're an atheist!"

What I really wanted to say was, "But you cheated on me!"

"Yeah," he agreed, "but I've been thinking I might be interested."

I think what he wanted to say was that he wanted to heal us. It was a gesture; he believed in us. That big-hearted cynic found faith in us.

Our secret seemed so potent there, then. As if it had a life of its own, and if I didn't clasp my hands very carefully in my lap and keep my legs crossed just so, it might spill out everywhere. What neither of us said was that we wanted to regain control of a situation that had started spinning out of control. We agreed on so much. We agreed to pretend it had never happened.

"THIS PERIOD MIGHT have begun with you having a great deal of security—thinking that you knew what was going on, what was about to happen," the Astrologer said. "Then lo and behold, your whole world got shaken, making one of your greatest fears come true. 'Oh my God, I was blind. Oh my God, I got hoodwinked. Oh my God, I pulled the wool over my eyes' . . . Which is one of your worst fears, if not the worst fear. It's very humiliating for you." Shame entered my life.

I wonder now whether I was attracted to that particular cosmopolitan expression of Judaism precisely because it was what I aspired to yet was most incapable of.

My husband told me that I set standards for myself that I didn't live up to. I wanted to be good, moral, generous, diligent, loving, sensitive, loyal, dependable, reassuring, ambitious, successful, healthy, innovative, vibrant. I wanted to make a family, be a good daughter, a good friend, a good writer, a good provider. I wanted to find peace and stability in family life because my own family had been emotional mayhem. I wanted to be happily married. My standards were high; I wanted to walk with the angels.

But I had an affair. I ended my marriage. Dashed my own hopes (pulled the wool over my own eyes). I'm not an angel, and it wasn't a strategy—or a religion for that matter—that failed me. It was something in me, a disconnect between me and my dreams, some misunderstanding about what was right, about how to be good. A basic misunderstanding. But once upon a time, long before I admitted the flaws into my life, I thought religion might save me from them.

"EVERY REVOLUTIONARY," WROTE the theologian Henri Nouwen, "is challenged to be a mystic at heart and he who walks the mystical way is called to unmask the illusory quality of human society."

I read a lot of Nouwen while I was researching my book. He was the go-to guy for pastoral theology in the 1970s. His concerns are so dated now: he worried about Nuclear Man, the "threat of New Technologies," and hippies. But he was a great pastor and writer because of the resonant clarity with which he explained that ministering to people in need was ultimately about understanding what comfort was and where strength lies. I keep coming back to the idea that there's something fundamentally revolutionary in compassion.

I called Temple Beth Elohim in Wellesley to ask if my mother and I could come to their High Holiday services. Apologizing for the last-minute call, I explained to the woman who answered the phone at the synagogue that my mother was very ill, critically ill, and that I had traveled from out of town to take care of her.

"Are you members?" she asked. We were members, I told her, twenty-three years ago; my sister and I had our bat mitzvahs there. I didn't elaborate on how disappointing it had all been for us. How forbiddingly clubby my mother had found the wealthy community, particularly unwelcoming to a recent divorcée and not especially well-equipped to serve single parents. I made a flimsy, obtuse reference to how we were grown up now and didn't live nearby.

"But you're not currently members," she clarified, and then told me that the services were open only to members.

Granted, most synagogues have this policy for the High Holidays. I asked if we could buy tickets.

No.

"Could an exception be made? It's quite urgent," I asked miserably, frustrated with my inability to be direct. I wanted to say that it would be my mother's last Yom Kippur. Instead, I added, "It's very important to us." She suggested that I try Hillel at one of the nearby colleges. "They often have community services." I had never in my life heard "community" pronounced as if the word itself were filthy.

I didn't know how to explain that we weren't looking for an adventure, that my mother's deteriorating body couldn't possibly bear a folding chair in a drafty function room, or a twenty-minute drive. I didn't argue that, at nine months pregnant and on twenty-four-hour call to my sick mother, I didn't have the energy to take us somewhere that would require the use of a map, that we were both scared, already ravaged, and needed to be at least somewhere familiar if not friendly. That I couldn't possibly spend the afternoon on the phone tracking down Kol Nidre.

"Do you have children?" she suddenly blurted out. The loophole. The open house policy of all thriving synagogues: young families shopping around for Hebrew school.

"I'm pregnant," I offered. "So there's children on the way."

"But you don't have any now."

"Not technically."

"Yup," she concluded, "I can't help you."

Overcome with anger, I hissed at her, "Well, I'll just have to find us a real Jewish community then, won't I?" I hung up as loudly as I could.

WHEN I ASKED my father what was so great about the Episcopal Church, his answer was that he felt welcome there when he needed it most: isolated, confused, and shattered by guilt after the divorce. His church was "a big umbrella." In no small sense, the fellow members of his church rescued him by sitting next to him, adding his name to the telephone trees, and arguing local politics with him at picnic potlucks.

Over the past few years, I've heard so many people say some version of this: "I believe in God, but I don't believe in organized religion." It makes sense; we are a country of individualists, people who don't relish the idea of being herded. Independence aside, though, I'm not sure I understand the point of a one-man religious experience. We are ultimately utterly alone. It's as much a curse as a gift. But we're not prophets, and we don't have to take to the desert to atone. We build communities to take shelter in them: churches, reading groups, support groups, labor unions, mothers for world peace. I don't think I fully comprehended the significance of my father's answer until I found myself out in that darkness, casting about for refuge.

My community on Yom Kippur was my mother and me, alone in that chilly shell of a home—her choking down half a teacup of broth and a spoonful of Percocet in yogurt and me standing over the kitchen sink wolfing down a rubbery slab of leftover mozzarella marinara. In our conditions, neither of us was required to fast, and yet neither of us had the stomach for food.

Atonement is just hunger. That's how I came to experience it—endless longing and a bitter emptiness. On Yom Kippur, atonement is folded into remembering the dead. For us, there was nothing to *remember*; we were in it, sitting together in her dimmed bedroom, the dead all around us, our shadows, their echoes, my dying mother, my unborn son, this twilight space between life and death.

"PLUTO," CONTINUED THE Astrologer, "is very intense. Pluto wants to end your life as you have known it, and he doesn't care about whatever your expectations and desires were for yourself. Your life just doesn't mean that much to him. He's going to come along and blow away your dreams. Pluto isn't very nice to humans . . . and all of this might be very discombobulating. This is all an experiment now, a passage, an improvisation. You have to go with it, see where it takes you. You don't really have a choice. Because if you're trying to follow the old road, the one you were on, well, it's gone. There's no more road."

•

LATE ONE NIGHT in Italy, as we were trying to navigate a snowy mountain pass and slipping and sliding and whooping with delight each time the heavy old unheated sedan made it over another crest, my husband—long before he was my husband—said to me: "You know, if we ever get divorced, we'll just have to get back together again. That's just the way it is." I felt uniquely loved in that moment.

I repeated the story to my mother one day while we were talking about family and, true to her often solipsistic nature, she replied, "Your father never said anything like that to me."

He didn't really love her, she said. He was too young, and she knew it. She knew that their age difference of eight years would be a problem. She didn't think he knew what love was. She didn't think he really loved her. He talked her into it, and she said she was convinced, "because he was a religious man . . . once." She didn't know what it was like to be religious like him, and she was seduced by the exoticism of it, the promises hidden beneath the layers of this mysterious creed. He grew up Catholic; he'd been to seminary; he went to church on Sundays. He believed in something bigger, he believed in family, and he understood the meaning of vows. But he broke them. He strayed. He had a long dark night of the soul, which in Christianity is often considered a rite of passage. So, was it religion or my father who'd misled her?

She had seen (as I had, as my husband once had) religion as a cloak of protection. What did any of us know? She was a musician, we were writers; we invented stuff. We attributed tremendous creative and sustaining power to the expression of faith. We were vulnerable to religion's promises because unlike my father, none of us had been brought up in the middle of it, we weren't necessarily stuck with it—its failings, inconsistencies, equivocations. When it came to planning a marriage, I think we all put a great deal of stock in the religious system. So I had a Jewish wedding and signed a *ketubah*, a beautiful hand-lettered contract.

One day just after we'd broken up I had a burst of courage and decided to do some research about Jewish divorce—an ancient provision, put into place mostly to protect people from being stuck with a barren partner. I read that we'd have to sign a *get*, another contract, in order to be officially divorced under Jewish law. One of the special caveats of a Jewish divorce is that you are expressly forbidden from remarrying each other.

Despite everything that's happened since, and how very far we both are from that snowy mountainside, I thought to myself when I read that rule, "Thank God I don't believe in that bullshit anymore." I know there's no more of the old road, but it was there once, and I was on it, and it is a part of me. I don't have any interest in letting the Jews and their laws, or Pluto with his destructive hacksaw, strip me of my dreams, even the old ones.

"IT'S A GOOD time to trust your faith," said the Astrologer, "because there's nothing much in the real world you can rely on. If faith doesn't work, go see art, look at things that are bigger than yourself and your universe."

I wasn't brought up religious, and neither was my mother— neither were her parents before her. That side of my family is historically made up of socialists, freethinkers, and artists. There's significantly more Jewish pride in my blood than prayer. My mother lost her mother when she was thirteen and turned to music for solace—that's the religion she brought my sister and me up in. We flirted with ritual over the years (especially in dark times), but our collective impressions of it kept falling somewhere between hopeful and suspicious. Our household was an artistic one; I've spent far more Sundays in museums than Friday nights in temple, including this last, recent incursion into Judaism.

Shostakovich's Piano Trio No. 2 is irreducible in a way that Genesis isn't—or so it seems to me.

MY MOTHER SPENT fifteen years not dying, and on that point she was unwavering to the end. In order to take care of her during the last few months of her life, my sister and I had to expend enormous energy agreeing with her that she wasn't dying. We shrank our worlds in order to be with her in the way she wanted. We stood in for the home health aides she kept firing because she wasn't dying, we nursed her, tended to the minutiae of her terrible exigencies, deflected the visitors and callers whose valedictory wishes smacked of resignation and betrayal.

In the very last month, I took refuge from the ruins I'd made of my life in Brooklyn in my haunted childhood home, ten months pregnant, nursing my mother, and alone with my sister. The way we'd started.

"She's been going on fumes for three weeks already," the hospice nurse told us.

"She's in denial," said the social worker. "You have to help her accept this."

"I can only think in black and white," my mother said one afternoon.

And then later that same night, she grabbed her oldest friend's wrist fiercely and said, "Shhh. Don't tell anyone. I'm going to get better."

"I can't stay for this," her friend told me early the following morning. She hugged me hard, got into her car, and drove off without looking back.

•

ABOUT A YEAR and a half earlier, my mother had approached my rabbi while on a visit to New York, shyly asking if he would talk to her about a Jewish burial. It was the closest she'd ever come to planning, or even admitting, mortality—aside from the promise we had made to her long ago that we would bury her with her down comforter so that she would be warm. It was an awkward overture to Judaism that she only felt comfortable making with me by her side—emboldened, I presume, by my own inflated sense of security. For some reason the meeting ended up being too difficult to schedule, and the conversation never took place. Before the year was out, she'd become too sick to travel anymore.

Although she never did learn very much about it, my mother was definitive that she wanted a Jewish burial. She wrote that much into her will, but didn't elaborate, tiring easily of the subject. When the hospice rabbi came around for a visit, she summoned the energy to ask again what a Jewish burial entailed, but then instantly lost interest. When the rabbi said, "What would you like to know?" my mother just shrugged. I think she wanted the hospice rabbi to tell her that it would be easier to die a Jew. But she was as Jewish as she ever would be, and she knew without asking that nothing was big enough to make it easier.

I believe she wanted to be taken care of, honored, buried quickly, cleaned, blessed, wrapped in white, deep in sacred ground, an ancient prayer, one repeated across the world: *Yit gadal, v'yit kaddash . . .* The Jewish communion of the dead—that strange, massive, and ageless pantheon of our dead. A Jewish burial has to happen quickly: properly, within a day or two. My mother slipped into a coma on Thanksgiving and died late that night. The funeral home assured us that we had some leeway with the ritual, as it was the Sabbath and we were so totally unprepared. As long as she was being tended to, prayed over, and in the freezer.

Getting into a Jewish cemetery as an unaffiliated Jew turned out to be as difficult as getting into the High Holidays at a tony suburban synagogue. My sister's inquiries at her local Reform cemetery—an elegant parcel of protected, park-like land in Western Massachusetts—proved quickly futile when we realized that it would take days on end to convene the temple board to petition them for an exception to the members-only rule.

The hospice rabbi had suggested the Baker Street Cemetery, vividly describing how the cemetery's sections were divided into synagogues, and unions, and Old World towns—there was even a Workmen's Circle section (my great-grandmother had dedicated her life to the Workmen's Circle). The map of the grounds was like an Isaac Babel story. To be buried there in Yiddish with those distant comrades would be like coming home for my mother. And so, the day after Thanksgiving, my sister and I bundled my baby and ourselves up as warmly as we could and set out for West Roxbury. Our high hopes were quickly dashed. The cemetery wasn't far enough off Route 128—a row of trees separated it from an auto dealership and a grotty shopping strip beyond that. It was a forbiddingly tidy and arid place, especially on that very gray, subzero afternoon. When I dutifully called the director of the graveyard to find out if there was even a possibility of putting our mother there, he gamely replied that we'd probably have to join the Workmen's Circle and make a plea for special dispensation to be placed in that section. I barely listened to his by now somewhat predictable response. We already knew that we hated it there, and it had nothing to do with anything beyond the fact that my mother would have hated it too. It was ugly.

The cemetery where we ended up, a beautiful historical forested hill right out of Amherst Center, was perfect—not at all what we thought we were looking for, and not Jewish, though there are Jews buried there—the renegades and secularists. Wildwood Cemetery hosts an eclectic crowd of locals, professors, and artists. A large statue of a bucking horse marks the grave right next to our mother's resting place up on a wooded hill, the perfect vantage point from which to watch a winter sunset. Behind my mother's plot, there is a swath of elaborate benches marking graves from the last hundred years, each lovingly and haphazardly arranged among the trees. Quirky affairs, like my mother: one bright white marble bench, guarded by leonine gargoyles and looking like something Salvador Dalí might have painted into the scenery, bearing the admonition "Watch It."

Meanwhile, I was on the phone with the funeral directors, trying to negotiate the hiring of a rabbi for the funeral. No slight matter, as it seems that especially on a Saturday morning over the Thanksgiving weekend, any rabbi worth his salt is either unreachable or unavailable. The funeral director finally ended our search for the perfect rabbi on short notice with the suggestion, "Look, I've got someone who can surely do the service for you; he's a local cantor who's always up for anything."

I wanted a rabbi worthy of my mother—someone who wouldn't patronize her, or us, by pretending to know us. Someone who could honor her with the simple ancient ritual that she had wanted. I wanted someone unique and brilliant, not freelance. But I was ever so wrong to equate freelance with unworthiness, or to underestimate what musicians, a cantor and a composer, can just *know* about each other.

Cantor Morton Shames called the next afternoon to talk about the service. When I told him that my mother was a complicated woman and that it was very important to us that he not pretend he knew her, he gently replied that he understood. For well over an hour, I tried to explain my mother to him, as if it were the most important portrait I would ever paint, miserably trying to sift the most salient details from seventy-two years of her life. My sister and I, independently, rambling on over the phone to this unfamiliar soft voice, both ended up describing my mother as an aesthete—so thoroughly consumed with the pursuit of beauty that often her feet didn't touch the ground. This held true as much for the music she wrote as for the way she arranged flowerpots in the corner of a room, as for the intent way she listened to her friends when they spoke. Cantor Shames interjected with quiet exclamations—"How wonderful!" "I wish I could have met her."

The funeral was not Jewish in the strictest sense, but of course, neither was my mother. It was not Jewish the way the hospice rabbi had explained a funeral, but it was the funeral she was meant to have.

As he stood by her plot on that cold, wet morning, flipping through a thick stack of index cards upon which he'd meticulously composed his sermon in pencil, it became utterly clear that no one but Cantor Shames could have honored our mother better. He understood her, through us, and what she meant to us, and that mattered. More than that, he seemed to have received, through means I'll never understand, a profound appreciation of her music. His voice, a bold, weeping tenor, cracking under the weight of the mourner's prayers, lifted to the sky. He blew the music up there and then carried her too, up past the treetops, and he took her away. She was really gone.

I AM A Jewish mother now, as my mother was before me, and her mother before her—Jewish, not quite Jewish. Another generation in the family that never really has found company in the house of the Lord. We're park dwellers: instinctual, undisciplined, two degrees isolated from the world we live in.

My mother was clingy, indulgent, petulant, and maudlin. Her love was demanding, sometimes contractual, almost unbearably consuming. "You should elope," she told us when we were planning our wedding. "Elope, but bring me." Throughout the fifteen years she spent fighting cancer, it was consistently impossible to get a straight report from her about her health; we'd have to rely on the most eccentric coterie of intermediaries for news. The good patches were fairy tales; the scary patches were often kept secret. When she'd get sick, my sister and I would come running to her side. Every time, whatever she needed. We were a small family. The three of us made it up as we went along. My mother taught me everything: to fight, to survive, to love for dear life. And everything that she taught me, my son has made me feel as an absolute, physical truth.

Isaac was named for laughter—that's his burden. When God told Sarah that she was to be a mother at 101 years old, she fell to the ground laughing, hilarious with disbelief. I wasn't supposed to be a mother this way either: too late, in the midst of a betrayal, a collapse, a long, painful death, the disintegration of my plans, ideas, dreams, this crucible of destruction. I wasn't supposed to be a mother like this. But Isaac was meant to be.

The moment of revelation is absurdly clear in my memory: I was sitting on the edge of the tub, washing clothes in a bucket. I adjusted the hot water and let it run over my hands, thinking that the only thing I knew was that I had to have my baby. I can't have been more than three months pregnant, and I was so profoundly confused about every single thing going on in my life that the sudden feeling of conviction was startling. My son was never a choice. Stopping the pregnancy was never an option, and how I felt about the baby was already more than how I'd ever felt about anything. It was love or truth, an absolute belief in the invisible. It was religion. Now I understand.

•

I UNDERESTIMATED FAITH. I looked for it in the wrong places, such mundane places—I looked for it in books, in rituals, in gatherings of people. But that's religion for people who have it. I hit the limits of that kind of faith the moment I strayed from the plan. It was all there; then it was dust.

The Astrologer says I'm not out of the woods; there won't be any order in my particular configuration of stars for some time to come. Pluto, Saturn, Uranus, and Neptune are all still lording over me, fighting for dominance. In my own gimpy, flailing way, I've been answering to all of them, and none. My son was born three weeks before my mother died. Time enough for her to see him alive; time enough for her to realize that seeing him wasn't enough; time enough for her to forget him and forget the sadness of losing him to the future; and time enough for me to watch my mother and my son exchange places. For three weeks, these two helpless, overwhelmed creatures had the same desperate faraway look in their eyes. They spent three weeks watching each other—time enough for eternity.

Stories I Tell My Children

I was walking through the flea market in Florence one day and there was a Gypsy dressed like a farmer who had an enormous rusty birdcage filled with kittens. I asked him if he had any black and white boy cats and he said of course he did and handed me a tiny little tuxedo with electrified fur and a lunatic expression. I named him Teodoro, Teo for short. Back home, he hid, then ate, and then became a kitten like all kittens—entirely hysterical. He raced from one end of the studio apartment to the other. He scampered the length of the top of a bookcase as if being chased by an elephant and kept running even after he ran out of bookcase and then crashed to the floor. He sprang to his feet indignantly, and streaked under the bed. He had none of the normal survival instincts; he heard coffee bubbling in the moka pot on the stove and took a running leap into the flame, burning off all the eyelashes and whiskers on the left side of his face.

I didn't have especially good instincts myself. I was twenty-one years old and it took me almost six weeks to figure out that Teo was a girl and by that time the formative psychological damage had been done. Amazingly, once I figured out that she was female, I started treating her differently—mostly with disdain.

It's not cute to burn off your face if you're a girl; it's idiotic. Girls should know better. I was disappointed because I wanted a boy tuxedo, and embarrassed because I didn't know the difference. I was fascinated by how differently I felt about her once I knew, how all of my repressed ambivalence and anger about everything was so swiftly projected onto her. Her ego got fuzzy, she started getting chronic urinary tract infections, and she only expressed extremely strong emotions. The vet told me to cook her risotto so she wouldn't get UTIs anymore—preferably with liver, which is very good for cats.

I moved in with my Italian boyfriend, who hated animals because they were hard to control, but he thought Teo was hilarious the way she hurled herself from one end of the apartment to the other, sliding helplessly on the supremely well-waxed wood parquet, ears flattened, claws extended—nothing to give her any traction, she would crash into the wall, the actual force of collision far louder than it should have been given her skeletal frame. He also thought it was hilarious that I had given her gender-identity confusion; he blamed her personality on that. But he didn't like the dander that Teo spread across the apartment, accumulating in the shiny corners faster than he could sweep. And he was jealous of the chicken liver risotto that his mother, Rosetta, cooked up once a week on Sunday afternoon and brought over to us packed neatly in Tupperware. He bought her an orange and purple collar with a number of bells on it, just to make her crazy. He cut a hole in the door to the balcony so that her litter box and her food dish wouldn't be in the house; he preferred it when she was out on the balcony watching birds.

Poor Teo was born into an identity crisis, and since she wasn't the cat that I really wanted—not a reincarnation of my childhood cat—I treated her unkindly. Which we think explains why she tried to fly away.

She'd been outside on the balcony with her food and her box, watching birds. Between the predatory instinct to chase them and a compromised sense of self, she had no idea she wasn't a bird or that she too couldn't fly. Why would she? The birds were racing free, past the prison of our balcony's iron railing. They were gods of speed and height and Teo wanted to be one—or she wanted to kill one. In one wild moment, unhitched by hesitation, she leaped and sailed past the iron railing. She took wing and then dropped.

Three floors down to the cement courtyard below.

We didn't know she was gone. Not for a while at least. But eventually, maybe an hour later, the vast silence of the apartment thickened. A low, almost-mechanical moan spread, it seemed, like a spill across the floorboards. Unmistakably Teo—and yet also not convincingly animal. I called her name and searched every nook of the apartment before I thought to look over the balcony rail, where I saw her, crouched in the middle of the courtyard below. Her eerie cry unwavering, unattached to breath or voice. From the balcony I could see the back of her head, still as a statue. It was a stillness I realized with horror that cats never assume. No ear twitch, no ruffled whisker. Her tail was tucked tight under her body as if dead.

I raced down the stairs and out the main door. When I picked her up she trembled violently for a moment and then released into my arms. I carried her delicately back upstairs. When I set her down on a chair in the apartment, she curled up and the moan in her abdomen finally quieted. She slept without stirring for two days in that same position. And then, simply, recovered.

MY CHILDREN LOVE to hear the story of Teo, the cat who tried to fly. They consider her escape a thwarted act of heroism. They tell me they can imagine her ears growing large like wings as she sailed across the sky. They like cat stories in general; cat stories are second only to my childhood Near-Death Adventures series.

For as long as I can remember, my mother carried her keys on a big round ring, like Saint Peter. When I was four, I thought it would be fun to play driving. We lived in Texas then and had a large stone ranch house in Granada Hills, an arid development outside of Austin. We drove all the time. You couldn't get anywhere except for the pool, the dam, the neighbors, or the rocky outlays behind the new houses without a car. My mother liked big, safe sedans—Oldsmobiles, Lincolns. My father favored projects: a '62 Rambler with an alignment problem that forced the car off the highway into the Dairy Queen parking lot every time we passed it; a '58 Cadillac that lived in the garage. When my mother made him get rid of the Cadillac, my dad swears that was the beginning of the end of their marriage. "Little deaths," he calls them—love deaths, he means, not sex.

I got a hold of my mother's key ring and, not having a car on hand, thought I might drive the house instead. The outlet in the living room looked convincingly enough like an ignition switch. I remember cocking my head to the right and making car sounds as I inserted one of the long keys into the outlet, and then the living room went sideways, the hues of the room shifted, thrummed, and my mother was over me and just behind my ear and running the length of the green-green shag carpet, arms outstretched.

It was a cleverly decorated living room: haute sixties. Shag carpet, low plush chairs that adults had to lean and squat to get in and out of, richly upholstered in red vinyl. There was a matching yellow vinyl ottoman. The chairs were on wheels and the ottoman spun around. Those features were the highlights of the room, as far as I was concerned. How far could you get the chair to roll by running and leaping? How fast could you spin yourself belly down on the ottoman? My mother waged a twenty-five-year war on those unruly casters. She was always coming up with new and better rubber stoppers to put under the wheels, to keep the impossible chairs from migrating. There were also fancy black leather side chairs that I recognize today as finely made designer imitations, and three mushroom lamps—all made in New Jersey.

My best friend, Kimberly, lived across the street. She was five too but could already do walkovers and had a white leotard with a diagonal stripe that looked exactly like an Olympic uniform. She was expert in making mean faces. She tightened up her mouth and narrowed her eyes to slits. It was really effective. And she never cracked. Our favorite game was *Masterpiece Theatre's Upstairs Downstairs*. I always played Rose, the eighteen-year-old chambermaid. None of us ever played characters from the upstairs. Our favorite, most hilarious joke was: Knock knock. Who's there? Petunia! Our secret word was *shnomershnahm*.

Her backyard bordered the perimeter of the development, and beyond the jungle gym and ornamental tree line there was a vast expanse of rocks and monkey grass. Our adventures took us out into the desert often. We had to watch for scorpions and the dense tufts of monkey grass—a single blade could impale your bare foot. One day we were out in the desert, tearing down the dirt trails to escape from a member of the aristocracy who'd gone crazy; we were on foot, Lord Chamberlain was on horseback. Even though I was slower than my little sister and Kim, I was in the lead that afternoon; such was my terror of Lord Chamberlain. As we made a mad break for the safety of Kim's backyard, I leaped wildly over a big stick lying across our path. I was aloft when I heard the rattle. I realized at once that the stick was a rattlesnake and my foot had landed within an inch of the deadly creature. I hollered and my sister and Kim took off in the other direction.

We kept a rattlesnake kit in our glove compartment and more

than once my father had meticulously explained to me (because he thought it was interesting) how to treat a rattlesnake bite by blocking the poison from traveling with a tourniquet, cutting an X into the wound *with a knife*, and then using a flimsy rubber thimble to suction out the poison. If you didn't have a kit, you had to suck the poison out with your mouth.

My sister and Kim were trapped on the other side of the snake, out in the desert. Even though I was shuddering with fear, it was up to me to save them. How quickly our lovely game had turned into a horror. I turned and ran screaming back toward Kim's house. I had to cross through a bramble patch, ford a creek, and cut through the tiny forest to get to the backyard. At every step I imagined rattlesnakes moving on my ankles. There were black bears too crashing through the trees after me. My sobs were deafening. There was no way that my sister and Kim would survive out there alone.

Kim's father, Al, was a pharmacist who rode a motorcycle and had a bushy handlebar mustache. My cries brought him out of the house. He heard "rattlesnake" and went to get his shotgun and then headed back through the yard toward the desert. I followed at a safe distance, picking through the grass with extreme caution. Night was falling rapidly and we could no longer hear the other girls screaming. Then Al stopped suddenly, took a shot at the dirt. He poked around in the grass with a nearby stick and suddenly fetched up the dead rattler, draped massively, limp, and headless. With a mighty gesture, he flung both the stick and the snake out into the desert.

My sister and Kim had meanwhile bravely found their way back home through the other neighbors' manicured backyard—the new neighbors had installed soft baby green yard grass deep behind their tall white house with its Georgian columns. We didn't know the new neighbors—they were all naturally blond and didn't use the free neighborhood pool. Mostly there seemed to be a lot of boys who lived there. Older boys who played mailbox baseball on their dirt bikes. One time when a bunch of them rode past, hooting and waving their baseball bats, my father lost his temper and stormed outside with his own bat. "Come on back here, you fuckers," he yelled. "What are you scared of?" He headed right out into the middle of the empty street, walking in the direction they'd gone, brandishing his bat and cursing. It was a cul-de-sac, so either he was going to bash all their brains in when he got to the end of the road, or they were going to escape off-road on their dirt bikes.

My daddy didn't have any intention of actually catching those boys. But they did scare. They stopped mailbox baseball but it wasn't long after that incident that my little sister went out one day to check the mail. She was too tiny to actually see into the mailbox. She could only open it by jumping and catching the hook and then reaching in blindly to collect the mail. That day her fingers fell not on smooth paper envelopes but on the half-dead body of a large crawdad extracted from over by the dam and left to cook inside our mailbox in the hot Texas morning.

Our mailbox was at the end of our driveway, which extended from the side of our house, which was set far back from the road on a rocky hill. Even though the large house faced Espanola Trail, you had to turn up the unmarked side street to get to our driveway. Our neighbors across the side street had a matching driveway coming out of the side of their house; our two driveways were like perfectly mirrored tributaries. Behind us, quite a way farther up the hill, there was a stylish A-frame. That family who lived in the A-frame had a lot of vehicles and a giant black dog. When their dog had puppies, the lady invited us children up to see them, scheduling the visit for when the mama dog was at the vet. The puppies were so cute, black and soft and floppy. I'd never held actual puppies before and was of course enchanted. But then the mama dog arrived back early from the vet and saw us children gathered around her children and before the grown-ups could realize what was happening she leaped out of the back of the pickup and bounded toward us, howling, growling, and barking. She reached me first and easily knocked me to the ground. She straddled my body and put her two front paws on my shoulders and barked and growled, teeth everywhere right up in my face. The grown-ups must have acted quickly because she was pulled away before she could eat me and I ran screaming back down the hill to my house and have never trusted dogs since then.

The hill is really the most important part of that story. The hill and the pickup. Because there was one time that my father borrowed the pickup in order to haul some wood he needed to build something. Hands down, the most exciting thing we could imagine was riding in the back out on the highway. Don't open your mouth! my sister and I yelled at each other and rolled to and fro as the truck turned into the lumberyard. Our wild rolling around must have disturbed my father, because on the return trip he made us ride up front in the cab, the two of us squashed into the passenger seat. Despite our protests, riding in the cab had its own excitements. We were high up and close to the windshield so we could see everything. The Dairy Queen flashing past. Our pink schoolhouse. The supermarket. The giant billboard that came up suddenly on the left announcing our development: *Welcome to Granada Hills*.

My father pulled the truck slant into our driveway, half in, half out, perched just a little dangerously on the steep road, and jumped out to unload the two-by-fours. My sister and I stayed excitedly in our tall front seat to continue our game of truck driver. My father waved at us that he needed to run inside to get something and he'd be right back so we could return the borrowed truck to the neighbors up the hill. It took me a few moments to digest that bringing the truck back meant that I'd have to face the dog and I didn't want to do that so I told my sister I was getting out. But somewhere between playing truck driver and kicking the gearshift while crawling over to get to the steering wheel, we had released something—like the parking brake—and the truck started to roll backward, slant, out of the driveway and down the hill. It gathered speed immediately and I could see my father running out of the house and toward the truck, arms pumping like a professional racer, growing smaller through the windshield as we were sucked backward. My sister and I didn't make a sound as we grabbed for things—handles, the stick shift, the rearview mirror. The truck sped backward into another neighbor's yard and the rear wheels pitched at once into the gravel pit at the corner of their lot. All of the houses had gravel pits. It was as if the developers had built the houses and then fled, leaving a grid of provisional front and backyards behind. My mother screamed from somewhere and the front wheels of the truck left the ground as the whole truck bounced toward vertical. Then froze midair. There was a loud creak and the truck settled upright into the pit. It took another borrowed truck and a lot of chains to haul that truck out of the neighbors' front yard. But we were miraculously unharmed.

A number of homeowners along that stretch had installed grass or even shady trees to make a front yard. Only our white stone house stood nakedly on a rock plot and my parents, both city kids, never considered buying the grass turf that arrived on delivery rolled up like expensive wall-to-wall carpeting. Instead they bought baby fruit trees and planted a garden up behind the house. I don't know what actually grew there, but one late-October day, my mother sent me out to find a pumpkin and by some divine intervention, I found a large, perfectly round pumpkin, grown as if overnight, and to my great delight just in time for Halloween. For years, I was convinced we had a magic garden in Texas.

The front yard was patched with thirsty brown grass, large

white stones, and sand. One day, my sister and I discovered a truly enormous red anthill in the front yard by the stairs. Of course we ran to tell my father so that he could get his vaporizing poison. Red ants bite and we knew better than to ignore their incursion. Daddy asked me to show him where the anthill was and I led him out front. As I stood in the warm sand, wiggling my toes in an abrupt section of softness, I narrated to him in great detail the size of the colony, how there were so many ants crawling over it that at first we had thought the earth was alive. My sister shrieked then and my father pointed at my feet. "You're standing in it!" The warm sensation on my feet and legs, like a drowsy blanket of sun, was thousands of red fire ants massing up my legs. My father sprung into motion and, taking me into his arms, raced back into the house, calling to my mother as he ran to start a bath. There were so many dead ants floating off my body I couldn't see the water.

Once a scorpion crawled into my father's shirt. I saw it moving under the fabric. But he was lucky and got out of the shirt before getting stung.

MY MOTHER HAD childhood stories too that she told us when we were little. My favorite was about the time she found a whole box of expired candy bars in the trash behind my grandfather's store. She was very little, around five years old, when her father had a grocery in Philly. She was not allowed to eat candy. But she couldn't walk away from the treasure trove of sparkling chocolate bars in their wrappers just sitting there, perfect. So she decided to distribute them to the other children in the neighborhood who were allowed to eat candy. She felt like royalty handing out the riches. No one would ever have to know!

Not an hour later, my mother's favorite friend, a little black boy named Pookie, was back in the store. His grandmother had him tucked under her arm. She stormed up to my grandfather (who had no idea what was going on) and wailed, "You fed my Pookie worms!" She grabbed her boy by his ankles and turned him upside down. She pumped him wildly in the air trying to get the rotten food out of his body. "You gave my Pookie wormy candy!"

My grandfather, quick to judgment, concluded that Pookie had helped himself to the candy from the trash and accused him of stealing. My mother couldn't stand by and let Pookie be punished for what she'd done even though she was only trying to do something nice. So she had to fess up. And she was punished. Of that you can be sure. But her conscience was clean.

I CAN REPEAT my mother's stories to my children but they will never know how she spoke so quietly as she told them, you had to lean in to hear her. How she held her chin aloft except when she was eating. How the light caught the soft cut of her cheekbones and her tall forehead, her startling blue eyes, so often diverted because she was shy. How she stood straighter and widened her eyes when she caught a glimpse of her reflection in a window. The way she smelled, like water and pencil shavings. How proud she was, how vain, how beautiful, how quiet, how difficult. Loyal, cowed, intent. She had a wonderful sense of humor but wasn't funny. She wore regret. She wore regret when she ordered ten slices of ham at the meat counter. There was regret in the way she wrote out a check at the cashier.

They will never understand what it was like to move through the world with her. The evening we went to Bloomingdale's together right after she'd started her first-ever course of chemotherapy because she wanted a cream that smelled nice and that was fancy enough to feel like compensation. I was along to egg her on because my mother never frequented department store makeup counters. She knew the prices would make her cringe. She had in mind to buy Shiseido—because after many years she'd finally used up an old jar of Shiseido cream that my sister gave her that smelled nice. But the woman behind the counter steered us away from Shiseido toward the products that older women wore—Lancôme, Clarins, La Prairie. The woman selected a cream and began talking earnestly to my mother about "free radicals" and rogue toxins. Had we ever heard of free radicals? she asked, and my mother grimly nodded. My mother glanced at me and I knew she was thinking about CAT scans and contrast liquid and the rogue toxins coursing through her bloodstream strategically targeting cancer cells in her lymphatic system. The woman launched into a long explanation of how the cream she was showing us isolated and drew out toxins from the skin's surface, like a magic magnet.

There was an abrupt shift in the dynamic. My mother unexpectedly began to feel superior and gracious toward this poor over-groomed woman who was rehearsing a snake-oil pitch that, despite her best intentions, sounded asinine to a cancer patient. It was a shift during which my mother decided that she didn't need a perfumed cream that cost too much and that, gracious as she was feeling, she didn't need to listen to the sales pitch anymore. She interrupted and began to walk away, pulling me gently along with her. At which point the woman became desperate. "Ma'am," she called out urgently. "You must never use soap on your skin. You are dehydrated. Did you just lose weight?"

I laughed cruelly—it just came out like that. My mother had never used soap a day in her life. Months would pass in fact in our house in which there was nothing more than a brittle bar of kosher soap behind the dish rack in the kitchen for the bamboo salad bowls and crystal wineglasses that didn't go through the machine. My mother didn't think about soap.

I was a little unsettled by a sense of shame for not having

protected her better, for having blithely led her into this carpeted unreality. As we walked across the mall parking lot toward her car, I realized too that the lady in the store had thought my mother was much younger than she was. She thought my mother was a middle-aged woman with dehydrated skin rather than a sick elderly woman with astonishing, untouched skin.

THE PROBLEM IS I don't know where Teo the Flying Cat ended up. I had to find an emergency foster home for her when my Italian boyfriend dumped her one night on the steps of my mother's house after we broke up. "It's too painful for me to keep her," he wrote on a note taped to the cage. And I don't know where my Italian boyfriend ended up either. He doesn't show up on Internet searches or social media, which doesn't make sense because he was the kind of guy who would have loved social media. Which God help me I think means he's dead.

The problem is I'm still scared of dogs. The problem is that I can tell my children about my mother chasing us through the house in Texas brandishing carrot sticks and singing, "Orange horsey food . . . come and eat your orange horsey food!"—but I can't tell them the sound of her voice, or the warmth of her body. How happy it made me to hear her laugh. How she cried over spilt milk all the time. The problem is that I'm not sure the little boy in her story was named Pookie but I am sure that he had a silly-sounding name, that his grandmother said, "You fed my boy worms!" and that she held him upside down by his feet. I am sure that my mother still felt ashamed of herself when she told that story forty years later. But the problem is that I can't double-check the name with her, or anyone. None of the people from her story are here anymore. I have barely the ghost of a story. The problem is that nothing grew in our garden in Texas.

Landslide

Beppe was an outlaw and it was the first thing that made me fall in love with him. He was maddening, profane, passionate, broken, and so very neurotic. When the morning sun cracked the shutters in the bedroom, he would raise his fist and curse the day: *"Porca puttana! Madonna troia. Mincchia che sole di merda."* Dust balls gave him stomachaches and we had to polish the chrome fixtures in the kitchen and bathroom after every use. He had expensive taste in clothes and ate and drank too much. Sometimes I could hear him hollering behind the bathroom door. He had faults and virtues in wild plenty, but I never forgave him for refusing to give my mother a blanket one night when she was cold in our guest room. He didn't think it was that cold. After we fell asleep, she snuck into the bathroom and stole some towels to cover herself with. How could I stay with him after that?

When I left my college boyfriend, Yates, to go out with Beppe in the first place, Yates told me that I was being controlled by hidden psychological motivations: He was my mother and Beppe was my father. Somewhere deep in my psyche and according to eternal laws not necessarily borne out by truth, I knew my mother's heart was secured, and I would perpetually be in pursuit of my father's. It wasn't just that Yates was right—Yates was sensitive and brilliant, he was always right—it was that at twenty I was *supposed* to be leaving my mother and her avatars behind. I was individuating, turning into an adult. The psychology of my love life was simple then in retrospect, the year before my mother's cancer started.

WHEN I TOLD Dr. Wilk I'd consulted an astrologer, she threw her hands up in the air and said, "Well, I guess you don't need me anymore, you have an astrologer."

Putting aside for a moment the sheer panic her comment ignited—and whatever pathology is revealed by my fear that my therapist might be insulted or angry with me—I hurled myself into an explanation. What I had experienced in the hands of the Astrologer was complementary to, not a substitute for, Dr. Wilk. The Astrologer had brought me solace. He'd told me my whole story from another angle. He didn't know anything about me, so he got lots of details wrong—I had cats, not dogs; I didn't go to the gym, I went to yoga; there was no water cooler in my office and my mother hadn't been called Mrs. Proctor since 1974. But his story wasn't in the details, it was specifically, intentionally, in the broad strokes. When he told my story, it was more than just facts that changed; it was the entire perspective. He zoomed out and I could see myself as a small figure in a black box, racing back and forth from one wall to another. It was as if he'd taken the whole theater of my life, lifted it wholesale, turned it thirty degrees, set it back down again, and invited me to look at it "this way." There was no magic, paranormal circus trick. Just a different perspective that, at least for a time, took the pain away. I was Pluto's plaything; it wasn't all on me.

The only other experience before that I'd had with a psychic was a low-rent palm reader on Via della Vigna Nuova in Florence. I couldn't have been more than eighteen and I was out with three friends. Over dinner, Chrys had been telling us about her mother's psychic, on whose advice they would change plane tickets if dates were misaligned. Chrys was not a person who suffered fools, but she gave the psychic leeway. Her mother's psychic had predicted her father's sudden death five years earlier—as if knowing about it beforehand made a difference.

The three of us were strolling around downtown after dinner, and we happened on a palm reader, who'd set up his little card table in the shadow of Palazzo Strozzi. Speak of the devil. We were a little tipsy and it seemed clear that after our dinner conversation, we couldn't *not* get our palms read. I was, however, ferociously skeptical and elected to go last if at all. I stood off to the side, smoking, chatting, and dancing with my skepticism, watching as each of my three friends had their palms read and reported back in turn. I remember he told Lilla that she was going to help people, maybe go to work at a nonprofit, and he smiled at her. Lilla has always had the most magical smile in the world and in the moment he smiled at her, and she smiled back, it was as if he synchronized with her radiance. He told Chrys that she would be involved in social justice, and he soothed her smartly and efficiently. He flirted wildly with Jolita, who flirted back, and I don't remember what he told her except for that her life wasn't going to look like anyone else's—he was on the money about that. I hesitated before taking my turn, and in that moment of hesitation my braggadocio evaporated.

I was shivering as I gave him my hand, and the few mono-syllabic words I tried to say in response to his questions tumbled haplessly in my throat. I was suddenly as frightened in that moment as I would have been if he were threatening my life physically. But why? He started by telling me sternly that I was lazy and would have to work harder for everything. And then he turned my hand over, this way and that, poking briefly at the creases in my palms. His face darkened. "No," he said. "That's all. I don't have anything more to tell you." And he turned deliberately away from me.

We were so young then. It would be years before any of us arrived at our future.

IN THE MORNINGS after dropping off my children at school, I go to a coffee shop on Seventh Avenue. Today, as I was beavering away trying to build a Venn diagram of how Shame Theory in psychology relates to the principal of Shame in the creation myth (of Abrahamic religions—a precision that the Internet reminds me to have), a nice young woman came in and warmly greeted the man who often sits at the spot catty-corner to where I sit. He always looks grimly at his computer, as I do—or, at least, as grim as I must look working on my Shame equation—and has a pair of impressive-looking headphones that I covet; they are pillowy and sleek, cordless, with a mouthpiece that extends space age from the left side. He wears them aslant, one ear on, one ear off, comfortable, as if he's been wearing high-end professional grade headphones for his entire life. As he releases this nice young woman from her hug, he explains to her that he's doing stand-up comedy now and comes to this coffee shop to write his routine. Now I can't keep my eyes off him as he works. Why won't he smile then? He's stony. The face of an accountant. Inscrutable, unsmiling. Is that how a comedian works? I've often suspected that funny people were hard, unseducible, untouchable. At least, they never liked me. For years I thought it was because they were all Scorpios and Libras, but it turns out to be something else. Whatever the particular chemical resistance, I can't perceive it in the man across the table. I have to conclude that he's not a funny stand-up comedian.

IT's TRICKY TO talk about shame. In the sphere of psychology, shame is tightly associated with narcissistic disorders. Shame in the hands of narcissists gets wildly perverted and expresses as an inability to understand anyone else's pain. If you're not on that spectrum, therapists tend to think that you really mean *guilt* and rush to reassure you. In religion, shame is fate and impossible to recover from. Like being expelled from the garden, or caught looking backward at Sodom. But shame is the betrayal of the self, and the most painful disappointment I've ever endured.

THERE ARE THINGS I've been able to piece together about my mother's life but there are a more significant number of unanswered questions. She was secretive and romantic, and had a remarkably complicated emotional life. I was a grown woman before I learned that my mother had been married before my father. My godmother let it drop one night when we were sitting around gossiping and drinking white wine. "Your mother has always been that way."

The most wonderful thing about my godmother is that she loves to pronounce: "You have always been that way." "Your sister was always like that." She's often wrong and will admit as much if you challenge her, but she's more likely to repeat the pronouncement than remember being chided.

"Your mother was like that with your father and just the same way with her first husband." I don't remember the specific indictment—probably something about my mother expecting to be treated like a queen and retributive when she wasn't. But I was too shocked to focus on the quality of the insult. *Her first husband.*

I couldn't believe that in thirty years of living with my mother I didn't know that she was married at nineteen and that the marriage was annulled. Annulled so completely that there was no trace of him. And once I learned about it, she still wouldn't discuss it. She only really talked to me about him once. His name was David and he was a film editor in New York. She married him so that she could get out of her father's house and come to New York, study to be a musician at Juilliard. He loved her. They broke up. She hurt him. When she did finally open up a little to talk about him to me, she told me that she had been horrible to him and regretted it.

In hindsight, my mother and my godmother had been friends a long time, but not so long that she had ever met my mother's first husband. Anything that my godmother knew about him, including the way my mother may or may not have mistreated him, she would have learned *from* my mother. And so whatever off-kilter, gently insulting pronouncement she made in the way that she did must have originated somehow from my mother herself.

THERE WERE ONLY two occasions ever when my mother sat down and told me, formally and for the record, stories from her dark past. The second occasion was only weeks before she died, during a flash of cogency and without any preamble; she told me about her mother's story and her father, and her grandfather, and recited names of relatives that she had never seemed to be able to recall before. She gave me a comprehensive genealogy. I was entirely unprepared, and I scribbled the information on the back of an envelope that was handy on the coffee table. I thought I would be able to reconstruct it later from my notes. But then I ate a whole bag of raw broccoli and went into labor the next morning and I lost the envelope and forgot everything she said.

The other time she talked candidly about her life was when we sat for a recorded interview the summer I was researching my father's religious journey for my book. I'd learned so much about him and she was jealous of all the diverted attention. So I sat down with her and my tape recorder and we had a monumental conversation during which she told me seemingly everything.

It is one month short of ten years since she died and I've been dragging around with me the cassette tape of that conversation ever since. I've been scared to listen to it. Scared that it would hurt to hear her voice, or that the tape itself had disintegrated over the years from poor storage, or worse, that I'd forgotten to turn the tape on at all and that I had no recording whatsoever of my mother talking. At last a friend offered to transcribe the tapes for me—he was trying to break the spell, help me find out how the story ends.

So many years of dreading the tapes: the transcripts arrived and it turns out there was nothing of what I'd wanted there.

Every part of the conversation that I had remembered, every part I wanted confirmed, had occurred after the tape ran out. The recorded conversation instead captured a long and fact-poor account of my grandparents' heritage and religious upbringing. Interesting, much of it—hazy details about the glove factory in Williamsburg, the grocery in West Philly, the dramatic divorce of the grandparents in the shtetl, the trip over in steerage, the family left behind in Warsaw—but it wasn't what I was looking for and none of it was the stuff I was scared to hear but desperately wanted to know. In other words, everything I will ever know about my mother's first husband, how she fell in love with my father, about the Norwegian composer and the secret married sculptor, who was the love of her life, was revealed to me that one time, after the recorder clicked off.

It had, after all, been a long conversation. The light streaming in the window over her desk had moved expressively over the course of the distended summer afternoon. All the clarity, the bright beams with dancing dust particles, had come during the first half of the conversation, the factual part that ultimately contained only the vaguest facts and was the prelude to the revelation, the confession—whispered in the rosy dusk, every syllable round and open—that came later. I think maybe that it was the only time my mother just sat and told stories on herself, and for some reason, the only time that she didn't implicate me somehow in her own life's reverberations.

I felt I was entitled to the stories but an interloper nonetheless. After all those years of conditioning—Don't repeat my mistakes; don't get married; don't tie yourself to a man; don't disappear behind a man—I realized that there wasn't a conviction she held that made sense in the context of her life, or mine. I also saw for the first time—in a way she'd never said explicitly—how tightly our ways were aligned.

That afternoon, I was tracing the affinities backward, unpacking as I listened: her first marriage . . . why she responded with such disappointment when I announced at eighteen I was moving in with Joey. The feeling of exile when she was *just a faculty wife* in the later years of my parents' marriage. For the first time, she wasn't burdening me with the consequences of her own life and, like a junkie, I rushed into every detail, looking for clues about who I was and why. There was a Norwegian composer, a visiting guest artist at Juilliard who was very attractive and dating one of my mother's friends. She had an affair with him and hurt the friend and her first husband. Soon after, her father handled the annulment, made David disappear. She tried to get him back later but he was too hurt. None of it entirely made sense, of course, because she told these stories about herself in a fragmented, secretive way. They were shameful. She didn't want me to know. She didn't want to think about it, utter it aloud. She spoke quietly, obscurely, and occasionally bitterly, that day. She often ducked her head, looking away, and I moved around the room, sitting across the desk from her, pacing, stretched up on the circular stairs that led from her study to the little garret room upstairs. She revealed so much more than she ever meant to, while I swaggered restlessly, so full of love, hope, and self-interest, so naïve about myself that I didn't catch all the details, didn't ask all the right questions—and didn't put in a new tape when the first one ran out.

After my mother died, maybe five years after that afternoon conversation, I started reading a journal I'd found in her desk drawer. It was just a small spiral-bound notebook she'd kept during a trip to Spain during her Fulbright year. On one page she described her train ride across France from Italy, the passing landscape. On the next page was a half-finished letter to her first husband. She begged forgiveness, told him she understood why, after so many times she'd come running to him and then run away again, he wouldn't even want to hear from her. She wrote that he was the only person she could trust, whom she knew now she loved, and that she'd been a fool . . . On the next page, I found a love letter, inchoate and passionate: She was going to Spain to be alone, to extricate herself from this other man and their doomed affair. She can't stop thinking of him even though she must. Pages on, she walks the streets of Barcelona and everywhere she turns she thinks she sees him, she hopes she sees him, not even the sublime beauty of this city compels her from the fever of him. Then she writes her estranged husband, then her lover; there are postcards taped in the middle, written to her father, cheerful, short, inattentive. I read it all in a kind of breathless stupor. There was so much anguish in the pages: regret and self-recrimination over her husband, guilt and frustration about the married lover, such insensitive hiding from her father. And a kind of blind, hapless faith underlying all of it— faith that things would work out, that she was more forgivable than she was, that she had more power and resilience than she did. No matter what she'd done to dissuade me over the years, I was fated to relive my mother's life, to carry shame with me forever, as she had.

DOCTOR WILK ALWAYS argued the point, "You are not destined to live your mother's life. If you're so scared of it, just decide not to." Doctor Wilk knew me so well and knew that what I needed most in the world from her was love and constancy. I didn't need to be fixed. I was unfixable. I needed to be embraced. The Astrologer put it another way. "If I were your shrink," he said, "I would be trying to cure you, break you of your pathologies. But I'm your astrologer, so instead I commend you on how you've resolved things about your-self that you can't change."

The Astrologer also told me that one day I'd get my faith back. In order to do that, I need to figure out where shame fits in. Which is how I ended up trying to build a shame diagram for Lot's wife, who was turned into a pillar of salt when she looked back upon the destruction of Sodom and Gomorrah. Some readings attri-bute to Lot's wife regret for leaving sin behind—that she looked back, and was punished, because she wasn't capable of moving for-ward. She couldn't head into God's future because she didn't want to abandon her sinning ways. More generous spins have her not wanting to leave her sinning daughters, and it was for them that she looked back. But I think she was hesitating. Trying to gather her life into her heart and her memories, because flawed as they were, they were hers and why should she detonate and run—as if nothing had preceded this moment? If only we could love the unknown—salvation—how fleet our feet would be racing on the path toward the future and divinity.

Unlike her husband or his uncle, Lot's wife was not a prophet or a god. In the cosmology of the Old Testament, Lot's wife was not a symbol of great faith. Rather, she is the exquisite human tragedy, fated to bind her heart to what she knows even as that same fate is condemned and blown to smithereens. Looking back is a singular gesture.

Whether it's regret, second-guessing, retrospect, hesitancy, fondness for the familiar, analysis, or simple nostalgia; look back and you get stuck. You can't look expectantly in the wrong direction and move forward. Lot's wife looked expectantly in the wrong direction. For me too it seems impossible to look away from the past. How can you? No matter whether you sinned horribly or walked with the angels.

IT SEEMS FUNNY to think that in the wake of my self-immolation after my mother died and when I was divorcing and having my first child, my greatest challenge was that I wasn't sure that I existed. And it's probably safe to say that I was right. The person I was had gone down in flames. My mother had been sick with cancer my entire adult life. If her illness wasn't in the foreground—an immediate, urgent concern—it was in the background, coloring entirely my relationship to life. I went from being a teenager who lived each moment with the reckless conviction that nothing is forever to being a young woman who bargained at every turn, weighing everything against my mother's health. I worked a lot; I worked hard; I worked steadily. I waged a battle against failure as if it were a mortal enemy—while cooking dinner, in yoga class, line-editing translations, balancing my checkbook. But when my mother died, the negotiation was over. My not failing—if such a thing were even attainable—couldn't save her and I didn't know how to be an adult anymore, I didn't know how to be me. So, no, I didn't exist.

SELF-DECEPTION IS YOUR greatest humiliation, the Astrologer had told me. The stars may have been pushing and pulling at me, but I was the one who had betrayed myself. Choice and free will were always mine. Still are—play your cards badly and you self-annihilate. The odd, unexpected card that comes up for me is that of the Fool—in Tarot, he is actually a wild card. It's a card of innocence and misstep. Upright, it can symbolize moving into the future, adventure, newness. Upside down, recklessness or stagnation. There are variations to his iconography depending on the Tarot deck. He is most often seen walking toward or off the edge of a cliff, face to the clouds, oblivious. He occasionally has a small dog at his heels, yapping a warning. He has a white rose in one hand and a bag of his belongings in the other. There are mountains in the background that are said to symbolize everything that he has learned, that he is leaving behind. He dresses in bright colors, ill suited for a long journey or a pitch over a precipice, and he whistles.

On her deathbed, my mother told my godmother, "Minna will never be satisfied."

The Fool

In my second-grade class picture you can see evidence. Evidence that I attempted to stop having bangs by cutting them off, leaving me with a tiny irregular crew cut at the top of my forehead. Evidence of my grandmother, who had been dead a year but whose crochet dress I was wearing—robin's egg blue with a puzzling arrangement of lattices which meant that I had to wear a white undershirt with it. I was excruciatingly embarrassed by the undershirt, which was babyish. I was very pleased with the dress, because it was my favorite color, and completely oblivious to the class implications of homemade clothes. Evidence I was naïve. In the group, only two of us had elected to dress up for picture day and only two of us did not own sneakers. Everyone else in the picture is wearing sneakers; a vast majority of them are wearing red, white, and blue sneakers with a Nike swoosh. But I am wearing sensible brown oxfords with slippery laces, and Alex is wearing slick black leather dress shoes. He's also wearing a jacket, button-down, and tie. We both look delighted. Dressed up and smiling as if our faces might break.

Alex's face of course ran a legitimate risk of breaking. It wasn't used to the stretch; his smiling muscles were underdeveloped. He looked perhaps more like he was engaged in an ancient mind-over-body trick whereby a person forces his ears away from his face, back across his skull, pulling his cheeks and lips taut in a simulacra of smiling. More often than not, in the regular course of events, Alex glowered, his face a dark cast of steely determination, thick brows knitted together and lips pursed uncomfortably over the broad endless half tones of the English language. He spoke with an accent heavily inflected still by the Soviet Union. This was our bond, after all—more than the linty, shared expressions of *trying*, and our clothes from a trunk. Alex's family were Jewish émigrés from the USSR and I was a self-fashioned socialist, half Jewish, half Catholic, secular daughter of academics and we lived in a town made up of people who drove twenty-five-year-old German luxury cars and knew how to golf. People who thought that sneakers were sensible shoes.

As committed as I was to the cause—and to the principles of a fellow traveler—Alex and I did not bond. In fact, we repelled, like the wrong sides of magnets. At seven, he was a patronizing old grouch who couldn't be flirted with or flattered. And I was his rival for success. American success.

Being a boy, Alex was inherently and more outwardly competitive. If I wrote twenty words in my daily thought journal, Alex wrote thirty. He'd lurk behind me when I was playing Stratego, upsetting my concentration and probably sending signals to the enemy. During quiet reading time, he'd sit near enough so that I would hear him making distracting muttering humming noises, but not near enough so that I could see him without craning my neck. On the playground, he tagged too hard, swung the tetherball too fast, punched the air victoriously like a boxer electrified by adrenaline. He drew me into this bloodless battle despite myself. And if he perpetually held the advantage it was because he was ruthless and determined. Where I would have turned the other cheek, or even turned my nose up at this metaphysical rivalry, he needled me, baited me, took me by surprise, and sought out any opportunity to crush me.

IN THE FALL we made applesauce. I stayed in at recess to peel extra apples and win the helper prize. In February, David Walker's mother came in and taught us how to make maple syrup candy in the fresh snow. I ate more than anyone else in the class. I had read about maple syrup candy in *The Long Winter* by Laura Ingalls Wilder and was pretty soundly convinced I could eat my way back into the days of sunbonnets, long skirts, and travel by horseback. I threw up all the gooey maple candy as soon as we got back into the drowsy warmth of the classroom. After the snow melted we started studying spring, and with that, the harvest—which I knew all about. As I knew about making hay while the sun shines, leaving fields fallow for their own good, and adding just a little bit of vinegar to ice water so that you don't get a stomachache from drinking too much of it after a hot morning working under the hot Kansas sun.

For our science unit, we were each given a pea shoot in a plastic cup, which we labeled with hand-drawn name cards and placed in a neat row on the windowsill. First thing in the morning, we measured our pea shoots and recorded the results. Then we watered the sprouts, carefully recording the amount that we watered next to the growth chart in the journal. There were no specific instructions for pea shoot maintenance provided. We were only encouraged to move our plants in and out of the sun, experiment with different amounts of water, even talk to the plants—anything that counted as tending was recorded in our journals. We frequently compared our progress—whose plant was thriving and what was the secret to their success. As I knew quite a bit about cultivation from *Little House on the Prairie*, my pea shoot did well. Its stalk was firm, its leaves glossy green. Alex's plant did well too. Possibly because he came from an agricultural region of the Soviet Union, but I didn't know for sure, and the Jewish émigrés in the greater Boston area seemed generally to be quite well educated; they were dentists and pianists and scholars, not farmers. The farmers had come over in the generation before, like my Ukrainian grandfather, from places like Kiev. I can't for the life of me remember where specifically Alex was from in the USSR, but I would have remembered it if he were Ukrainian like me, which would have been a near miraculous configuration, to be Ukrainian like me and Jewish like me.

From Alex's point of view, our plants were in a dead heat. He observed my watering measurements and copied my windowsill placement. To my delight, my sprout grew steadily, often at least a quarter of an inch taller than the plants of my classmates. Not because I was competitive, but because I wanted to own the farmer part of me. And then at recess one day, two girls came up to me at the jungle gym and reported that "Alex was inside and he drowned your plant."

The announcement was made with the urgency of a crisis. There were rules being broken, an attack under way, a *project* in peril. The three of us rushed together back into our classroom, which was quiet, empty, and dark, as it always was at recess. They pulled me over to my plant sitting on the windowsill, cheerfully clustered with five or six others. One girl kept her hand on my shoulder to soothe me, and the three of us gasped in horror when we saw my pot filled to the brim and a large expanding puddle flecked with soil on the windowsill around it. A stream of water and dirt had reached the edge of the sill and was slowly but steadily trickling onto the floor. The bell rang signaling the end of recess. The lights in the room came on suddenly as the teacher entered, the rest of the students pouring noisily in behind him. My hearty little plant, unmoored, listed soddenly to the side. I burst into tears.

THE OTHER DAY in the car, on the way to school, my children, Isaac and Anna, were clarifying for each other the difference between revenge and karma. Revenge is something that you exact upon someone for having done wrong by you. It is a gesture of anger (whether served cold or hot) and depends on an economy of pain: an eye for an eye. Karma is when the universe responds in kind to an act or behavior. An act of charity or generosity might bring you at some point something good. An act of cruelty similarly may bring you misfortune. Karma is dazzling because there is no linear relationship between what you do and what happens to you. There is no single actor involved. One man may deliver another man's karmic reward—but it may not be, and often isn't, an act of man but instead an act of nature, God, or circumstance. The timing of the behavior and its reward may not even line up—in some faiths karma arrives in the next life, in others it may come even before the misdeed is committed—because time in the higher order doesn't necessarily operate the way we understand it. Time folds upon itself, or swirls, every moment occurring simultaneously. Revenge is mediocre by comparison, petty, a small expression of anger by one man against another. And what is that against the backdrop of the universe?

ALEX OF COURSE denied any wrongdoing at first. But when confronted with eyewitnesses, he crumpled. He'd wanted, he admitted, to have the biggest pea plant in the class. He wasn't trying to be mean; he was overcome by his own ambition. Our teacher, Mr. Shepherd-Blue, regained control of the room and encouraged us all to embrace the event as part of the *process*, an acceptance of the life cycle—the very cycle we were studying with the pea-to-plant-to-pea science unit. My plant had been overwatered. It was as simple as that. I added a note to that effect in my observation journal and the class all agreed to bravely face the scientific outcome on Monday morning. All the plants, the teacher suggested, might do well with a little extra water to carry them through the weekend.

CHILDREN LEARN EARLY how stories work: the hero, the villain, the impossible conflict, the insurmountable obstacle, the thrilling crisis, the transformation, the saving grace, the resolution. From once upon a time to happy ending. Make no mistake, it's learned.

When he was very small, my son was frightened of narrative movies. He was perfectly happy to spend hours watching monster trucks and backhoe loaders move back and forth through mud while ersatz country music played in the background and a voice-over actor used his best puppet voice to explain the functions and distinctions of backhoe loaders. He was also perfectly happy to watch nature documentaries, where inevitably at some point a fierce predator would attack, maim, and eat a downy, wet-eyed innocent. But it took me years to convince him that in story movies, he could be confident that everything was going to work out despite adversity.

"How do you know?" he would ask.

"Because it's that kind of movie," I'd answer. "It's for kids. It has to work out."

That wasn't good enough. He still didn't trust that there was a way stories worked, or that if there was, I could know for sure. What finally won him over was when I showed him a trick—proof that stories are all subject to a controlling authorial hand. In all the best children's books, I warned him before we started *James and the Giant Peach*, the parents have to die or be otherwise removed, in order for the adventure to start. Roald Dahl is especially chilling. Little James Henry Trotter was only four years old when one day his mother and father "went to London to do some shopping" and, of all things, "Both of them suddenly got eaten up (in full daylight, mind you, and on a crowded street) by an enormous angry rhinoceros . . ."

He grew convinced that there might be a greater plan, because he could see the evidence of the pattern (and its logic) plainly, not only in *James and the Giant Peach*, but in *The Lion, the Witch and the Wardrobe*, *The Wizard of Oz*. And so he began to believe grudgingly in narrative structure—though he still preferred the unforgiving, and strictly speaking amoral, world of a bloody nature documentary.

But I preferred the stories when I was little; I found great refuge in those tight moral universes. I imagined myself a character and every morning as I tripped down the driveway on my walk to school, I was setting out on an adventure. I was the hero; Alex was the villain; everything was going to be fine.

Once children are taught the way stories are supposed to end, they learn that real life is different, more complicated. There aren't clear-cut heroes or villains; there isn't just one obstacle; and not everything comes out in the end—sometimes you can't even see the end. We build a fortress for children and then tear it down. And yet this is not as futile or cruel an exercise as it seems. First, because stories introduce children to a circumscribed moral world—a lifelong shelter—and second, because it is through this process that children begin to learn about faith, the way it lurks behind curtains, shining and hidden, seductive and frightening.

•

ONCE UPON A time there was a cat named Max. He was a street cat, a fit, tiger-striped adolescent tomcat who was one of the pack of cats who came to eat leftovers off the stoop of our funny little house in Italy, which was wedged into a funny little mossy hamlet on the far side of the river from the funny little mountain village. His full name was Max Emergency. There were two black kittens, still fuzzy and unsure on their feet, who followed Max Emergency everywhere. They seemed orphaned, or misplaced—like all the cats in our hamlet—and Max was a loyal and natural caretaker. He nudged the babies toward the food we left out, stood guard while they ate, hissed at rapacious, trespassing cats who belonged to other stoops. In the morning, we'd find the three of them all curled up on the mat outside our door, their faces tucked into each other's warmth, a tiny landscape of quivering fur.

Max Emergency had one master and that was Fred. Fred was a large prepossessing long-haired cat who had evidently once been a house cat, probably left out in the country when his owners went away on vacation (a common fate for Italian cats). He may have come up in a life of domestic luxury but Fred was made to rule the street. He was pristine—no bits missing from his ears, no gummy eyes, his long hair was never matted; he walked with his tail erect and his senses on high alert. There wasn't a skittish hair on his head. Unlike Max Emergency and the twins, who depended on us, Fred could find a hot plate of spaghetti at any number of homes. Many people in the village called him Il Rosso because of his coloring, but over in our hamlet, we knew him as Fred. Max Emergency worshipped Fred.

There were people in our hamlet, weekend people, who thought of the cats as a scourge. They didn't like the way the cats all scampered underfoot, begged for food, or sat superciliously on high perches and followed your movements with their eyes. Some people thought cats crept into the cribs of sleeping infants at night and sucked out their breath. They couldn't understand why we tended to the cats—they didn't care to understand. The cats were a problem and needed to be exterminated. It was as inevitable as a predator swooping down on its prey. One night we found mighty Fred collapsed on our stoop, his fur matted with vomit, his breathing labored. He'd been fed arsenic-laced meat. It was a dreadful scene. Fred was in pain, and drifting in and out of sleep. When he came to briefly and suddenly, he seemed frightened and terrible sounds came out of his chest. We put him in a box with an old flannel shirt. Max Emergency never left him. For hours that night, Max Emergency stretched his long slender body out over Fred, lying still, purring and breathing deeply, as if he could press his own breath into him. Once Fred died, Max stayed for hours longer, curling tighter over Fred's body, as if he could keep his corpse warm. I thought of Max Emergency as a hero that night, but a fallen one, because he couldn't save Fred, and everything didn't work out.

IT WAS OVER fifteen years from the date of my mother's first diagnosis with precancerous breast cancer cells to her death. In the intervening time, she survived non-Hodgkin's lymphoma and lung cancer. She was a terrible patient, frail, scared of needles, argumentative, not forthcoming, and had an especially low pain threshold, but she lived much longer than she was supposed to have lived.

When her treatments ran out and the breast cancer had metastasized to her brain, the doctors sent her home and called in hospice. The doctors told me and my sister that it was a matter of weeks. But she was so stubborn it went on for months. People called her heroic. She kept trying to fire the hospice nurses and wanted to limit the pain medication because she wanted to know what was going on in her body. She could only ingest a couple of pomegranate seeds at a time or a spoonful of broth. Her eyes wouldn't focus, she barely spoke, and she only seemed to recognize me and my sister. The nurse cornered me in the kitchen one day and told me that my mother was scared, not heroic or stubborn, and that's what was keeping her alive. There is no heroism in cancer. The nurse told me that I had to help her not be afraid so that she could at last let go.

When my sister and I were little we went in to cuddle with my mother every morning. It was as if we had an automatic timer that roused us from our own beds and drew us to hers before the alarm went off so that there were always a few minutes to cuddle and then the three of us could ignore the alarm together. We did it for years, probably long after most children stop going into their parents' bed. It's such a strong sense memory, I feel my mother's warmth against my body to this day. When my daughter comes into my bed every morning, I wrap my arms around her and surrender to the drowsy, powerful continuity.

The nurse told me again that I had to comfort my mother; I had to get her to understand not to be afraid; to make sure she knew that I was there with her. Hold her the way I now hold my daughter. Tell her whatever she needed to hear in order not to be afraid.

THE MONDAY AFTER the drowning, we all walked into the classroom to find that my pea plant had grown enormous over the weekend. It was green and vital, easily five or even six inches taller than Alex's plant. Revenge. Karma. Botany. I triumphed over Alex. At seven, I learned that things worked out, that there was justice.

Years later, I would realize that it wasn't justice; it was theater. Mr. Shepherd-Blue had intervened. He'd messed with the laws of cause and effect, kept the moral universe orderly, and made a fantasist of me.

But for a time, I was a believer. He gave me that. I had faith things would work out. Monday morning would come. That there are heroes and happy endings. There is comfort for the dying. That you can whisper in someone's ear that everything is going to be all right, not to be afraid, that you are right there and you aren't leaving.

The Waiting Earth

... Come
erba viva nell'aria
rabbrividisci e ridi,
ma tu, tu sei terra.
Sei radice feroce.
Sei la terra che aspetta

—Cesare Pavese

When my mother first bought this house in Tuscany, I was crushed. It was so far away from the city, and nothing at all like the tony rolling hills of Chianti. The house was taller than it was wide and impossibly organized—you had to pass through one small room to get to the other, as if the whole house were one winding staircase. It hadn't been modernized since 1962 and was unheated. Despite being out in the country, it didn't have a yard at all. The whole hamlet of dark, narrow town houses had once been the quarantine barracks for the castle up the hill. We learned that from tracing the origin of a crest carved into one of the stones in the wall of the basement, dated 1192. Infested truckers, passing through, who couldn't be allowed into the castle walls, once spent the night in our house. I was nineteen when she bought it and immune to its charms. I didn't want to shrivel up and die in a remote peasant village in the mountains that smelled of must, curing meat, and wet decaying leaves. As if that were even a risk. I was being petulant. It was the only house she'd ever owned and she'd waited half a century to live in Italy.

Our village was set high up in the Casentino—past the leafy forests of Milton's Vallombrosa, with its brambles and Etruscan stone walls, wild boar, exploding fungi, and minor medieval ruins. Dante wrote Canto IV of the *Inferno* in a tower in a field that crested to the left just before you made the turn into our town, Strada. Charlemagne sacked the modest castle that perched on the hill above our house. The Della Robbia family installed their exquisite terra-cotta roundels in broom-closet-sized roadside altars throughout the region. Saint Francis threw the Devil off the side of a mountain at the monastery not far away. Pilgrims visited the monastery by the busload. And yet there were never many tourists, because you need a car to get out that far. Many of the old people from Florence or Arezzo who once summered in these mountains were dead or had bought modern beach condos in the south. Their children moved to the cities. Their dank, unmodern properties sit empty. Small factories fill the divots between hills now; the little valleys are always damp with mountain water runoff, chilly because the sun is only high enough to warm them two months out of the year. Eastern European immigrants, who work in the small factories making socks, light fixtures, wrenches, fill the houses left empty by the adult children of departed mountain farmers. Houses were cheap there, because nobody wanted one.

Except my mother. It was perfect for her. She put in an electric piano (the most expensive thing in the house) to compose on, covered the midcentury Formica with orange contact paper, and installed a Shaker candle chandelier that she'd ordered from the Cohasset Colonials catalogue. She bleached the dishes and cookware that had been left behind by the dead parents of the former owners and threw my grandmother's crazy quilts over two horrendous foam couches that she'd bought at the factory outlet store two villages away. She falsified a supremely complicated trail of documents, and called in several favors, in order to own and drive a car (no easy matter for a foreigner)—a twenty-five-year-old Lancia that was in the shop more often than not and eventually was crushed in the night by a rogue boulder rolling off a mountain. When I think of that house and its town, I think of the deep yellowy green of ivy creeping down wet stones, the hazy, shadowed horizon of a small valley, and the smell of damp dirt.

Every May, the day after her last class, my mother would board a plane for Italy. She'd spend the whole summer in our hamlet, composing in the morning, taking little drives or walks in the afternoon, eating tomatoes and vinegar, and when dusk fell, she'd walk across the little bridge into the main village and sit at the bar in the square, looking out onto the oversized granite loggia, where they held a market every Thursday morning. She usually had a Campari soda and talked to Mirella, the owner of the bar. The people of Casentino, the Aretini, have one of the most garbled and startlingly shrill accents in Tuscany, quite a distinction in a region known for being the heart of the Italian language—and Mirella was a big talker. She would talk and talk, commenting on her husband's coffee, the weather, her swollen ankles, what the boys in the hardware store were up to, whether there were blackberries up on the road behind the village, the upcoming cherry festival, and when she ran out of subjects, she'd start up again from the beginning, sometimes filling in the gaps between sentences with delighted nasal outbursts and vocalized sighs that sounded a lot like *zooom zooom*. Mirella was always a great source for information, assistance, caretaking. We'd go see her whenever we needed anything. She was devoted to my mother, and me by extension. I loved to ask her about recipes in particular, because she was a wonderful and proud cook, and would always manage to slip in an insult for everyone who did things differently than she did.

Mirella had a son, Andrea, who looked like a professional tennis player, polished, gracious, and handsome. At twenty-five, Andrea married his high school sweetheart, an exquisite woman with long dark curls and a porcelain Botticelli face. They were golden against a backdrop of squat, red-faced, fat-featured peasants—a kind of genetic upheaval. On their honeymoon, Andrea's bride had an aneurism and was airlifted to a hospital where they saved her life by a matter of seconds. Three months later a swelling on Andrea's upper arm was diagnosed as soft tissue sarcoma. In a cultural holdover from another era, the family kept the diagnosis from Andrea, telling him he had the flu. But Mirella came right to my mother. She called her long distance from the pay phone in the bar, the credits on her telephone card clicking down the seconds at an alarming rate. She begged her to find out what she could from American doctors.

It was the late 1990s and my mother had been, at that point, just declared officially "in remission" from non-Hodgkin's lymphoma. Lymphoma is tricky. Patients can respond well to treatment and be fully in remission—and then it can come back in a flash. She'd been through intensive chemo and was clear, but still emotionally very fragile and jumping at shadows; she was hardly out of the woods.

Throwing herself into Andrea's case turned everything around. Between consulting eminent doctors and approaching cutting-edge research facilities and trial studies, she did more for him than she had ever done for herself. She also found a way to *use* her own cancer—she gave her cancer purpose. Because she'd been sick, because she'd been through the system, she was uniquely qualified to support Andrea and his family. For months she researched and contacted doctors, tracking his large medical file as it zipped across the country from Boston to New York, Minnesota, Houston. She felt alive again, determined and hopeful. But Andrea's cancer was a monster and he died after six months.

My mother took Andrea's death and his family's grief hard. She wrote a piece of music in his memory and dedicated it to him on the score—something she never did. Going through her final, perfect-copy scores now, all these years later, I can appreciate how extraordinary that dedication was. Most composers dedicate vociferously. If a piece isn't commissioned by someone, it's written for someone. For some reason—perhaps because her only dedication was to a dead boy—I associate my mother's disinclination to dedicate her work to hubris. Too little, on the one hand, because, over a long career of composing without being recognized, she had convinced herself that her music didn't merit a dedication, that it might have been stealing somehow to put someone's name on work that would only ever be heard once, mid-winter, in the poorly lit concert hall of a suburban college. Too much hubris, on the other hand, because I wonder whether she didn't worry about polluting her music with mundane associations—people, performers, the politics of the classical music world. I love this subtle, virtually unidentifiable resistance she had to explicit language. If words weren't beautiful, unlockable, operating powerfully on several levels, they were better left unsaid.

THE WIFE OF the owner at the monument store in Amherst reassured my sister and me that our situation wasn't as unusual as we thought. Some families just took longer mounting a gravestone than others. The reassurance was kind and the two of us wanted more than anything to accept it. We gushed at the woman on the other side of the desk and told her how relieved it made us to hear that. But had we caught each other's eye while we were reassuring the monument maker's wife that she had been reassuring, we would have simulcast the exact same thought. This is shameful. How can two daughters fail so badly? There was no excuse for not having put a gravestone up over my mother's grave. It had been ten years.

Outside the shop, in the small patch of grass next to the driveway, my children played The Ground Is Molten Lava, leaping from one hunk of sample granite to another. My nephew, Silas, was the distracted referee. He's tall, skinny as a rail, frantically self-conscious—his jeans ripped just so, his dark hair falling in a perfect dark fringe across the side of his face. He alternated between half-heartedly scolding my kids for their noisy game and texting passionately on his phone. He was ready to leave. At twenty, he's the only one of the three children who ever met their grandmother, and he was very close to her. This errand was too fraught for him. There was an explosion of screaming when Anna fell into the Molten Lava and Isaac somehow simultaneously banged his shin hard on the corner of a hunk of granite. I excused myself from the small office and went outside to quiet the kids.

"Mommy, I found the perfect one for Grandma!" said Anna, running up to me and pulling my hand in the direction of a pink rock with a horrid metal plaque on it.

"I actually think this one is much better," said Isaac, gesturing toward a bird fountain. I was inclined to agree with him but it was all ridiculous.

"Can we go?" Silas asked impatiently.

"Do we have to have a metal plaque?" I asked when I got back inside.

"It depends on what you want to write."

"We know what we want it to say," my sister said. We've known for years what we're going to put on my mother's gravestone.

"But Mommy wouldn't want a plaque glued onto stone," I said.

My sister had come up with another plan while I was outside: "We can choose a raw boulder," she said, "and have the carving on it." She handed me the binder with all the examples in it.

It's perfect, I thought, and wondered how much it cost. The piteous joke behind this whole enterprise is that it doesn't matter how much more or less it costs, there's no money for it. I have an idea that we'll be able to work out an installment plan. One way or another, people have to be able to buy gravestones.

EARLIER THAT DAY, I had brought the children to the graveyard for the first time. Technically, Isaac would point out, he'd been there before, but he was less than a month old at the time and didn't remember much. Technically, I am in the same boat. I have vivid memories of the horse sculpture, the particular slope of the hill, and the constellation of treetops when you look up, but for the life of me I couldn't find my way back to my mother's grave. I couldn't even find the cemetery. The GPS kept leading me into the back parking lot of a nearby apartment complex that had the same name as the graveyard: Wildwood.

Once we found the cemetery, I couldn't find the grave. After driving in circles for twenty minutes, I realized I was going to have to ask directions. Anna balked at the prospect of going to the gravedigger's office. Which I understood, especially since, in true New England style, the gravedigger's office was located in what looked like Nathaniel Hawthorne's winter retreat, complete with a pumpkin on the porch and autumn leaves swirling darkly across the threshold. Everything turned truly nightmarish when even the old man couldn't find my mother's grave in his computer or on his paper map. He had no record of her and wondered if we were even in the right cemetery. Fortunately, I remembered the horse sculpture, which oriented him and we finally found her in the computer listed, horrifyingly, under my sister's name.

"Do we have to follow him?" Anna asked in a frightened whisper, as the gravedigger emerged, tall and gray, from behind his desk to escort us to the grave.

"It's the wild part of the cemetery," he answered. "I don't want you to get lost."

But even when we'd arrived in the right spot—and there was the slope and the horse and the treetops—we couldn't find the grave. The gravedigger walked up and down, from one side of the footpath to the other.

"These old graves," he said, kicking at the ground.

"We don't have a stone yet," I said apologetically.

"It's all the leaves," he answered, and crouched suddenly to the ground. "Here we go. I remember I put a marker because you don't have stone." He swept a small pile of leaves aside, revealing a cinder block with my sister's name spray-painted on top. "I'll leave you to it."

THE THREE OF us stood huddled helplessly at the site. "What do we do?" asked Isaac. Always so reasonable.

"Well, this is terrible," I said. "Let's fix it."

We brushed off the cinder block and then began clearing leaves and twigs in the size and shape of a small cot. I told the children that we had to find stones to put on the block, because Jews leave stones on graves. We collected enough to cover my sister's name— that seemed like an urgent point. When we ran out of stones, we started gathering berries and twigs, acorns, pinecones, anything beautiful we could find. The longer we carried on, the less I could think of things to say, and then the children fell silent too. When we were done, we stepped back to consider our work. Isaac stood close to me and put an arm around my waist. "Mommy, I'm so sorry," he said softly. And Anna looked up, at us, at the grave, at the treetops, and, as if she suddenly understood, burst into great sobbing tears.

THE EARLY AUTUMN chill had burned off by the time we left the monument shop for the rock quarry. My sister and I had decided definitively against a formal headstone and wanted to choose a boulder to mark my mother's grave. It was a long drive. We left the shady part of the valley and emerged into a golden afternoon light. The office of the quarry closed early but we'd been told to go ahead and look around and mark the boulder we wanted for my mother with bright orange tape.

The boulders and gravel were deposited in two massive separate piles in a lot outside of the main quarry. Each pile was half a football field long and at least two and a half stories high. A small boulder came up to my knee; others were bigger than me. Each one distinctive. We saw grass patterns, and colors that seemed to come from outer space, mysterious veins, and miniature landscapes. We tried to figure out if my mother would want something oddly shaped or perfectly regular, stippled, or glass-like. We touched everything—gently, to discern with fingertips how smooth the surface, and solidly with our palms to figure out its temperature. Mommy, we thought, would love the beauty of a steely cool Brancusi slate. She would also love the warmth of an irregular slab of granite with green threads shooting through it. The sun, still strong but lower on the horizon, hit every surface differently. Some rocks absorbed it, some glittered, some deflected, others changed color in the shadows. They were golden and then rose. We found a formation far in the back of the pile that reminded us of Stonehenge; one upright stone took on a birdlike profile from one angle but, from another, was a walking man. We stopped and rested like lizards on smooth table rocks.

In the summer of 2000, my mother was working on a piece for voice and cello. She was stuck on the end and spent hours up in her study, windows closed, curtains drawn, trying to block out the noise of the hamlet. Our next-door neighbors could be raucous; they had all their meals at a giant table out on their back patio not ten feet from my mother's room. They turned on sports radio when they lay down for their afternoon nap. They bought a new power tool that summer and used it with unbridled dedication. The first year we were in the house, those same neighbors kept handing us plates of food through the fence that separated their yard from our front stoop. They worried that, as foreigners, we didn't know how to make our own. They also worried we didn't understand Italian, and so they yelled when they talked to us. In the summer there were always more people in the town, and more racket, especially on the weekend; their conversations drifting through the open windows and bouncing off the smooth stones of the ancient streets. The bell on the tiny church on the hill right above our house rang morning, noon, and night, resounding across the small valley, toward the church at the other end of town that to a different beat, in a different key, clanged back. As night fell, the cats, always underfoot, would fight and mate. You could set a clock by their yowling. By night my mother wasn't trying to work anymore, she would have joined the rest of the friends from the hamlet down on the street, at the long card table with the heavy white tablecloth draped over it where everyone gathered to eat dinner together, drink wine, and talk the hours away.

I arrived for a visit late that summer, not long after Andrea had died, largely oblivious to the battle my mother had been waging with the noise and with her closing melody. As we sat together on my first night, she turned to me suddenly as if startled, and grabbed my hand. "Minna, the most wonderful thing has happened. I must tell you." Her soft cheeks were flushed from wine and overripe tomatoes. "I figured out the ending." She liked to use pauses in conversation, to extend the drama, to add weight with timing where mere words wouldn't do. While she let the suspense crest, her eyes sparkled with anticipation—as if she were a small child who couldn't wait to tell me a secret but had to count to ten first, as if she weren't the one controlling the unbearable delay. "The bells," she finally blurted. "The interrupting bells."

WE COMPARED EACH rock in the boulder mountain against our mother—what she would have liked about it, what she would have noticed, what resembled her, what complemented her, what we wanted for her. She was there somehow, just under our fingertips. We were praying as we touched every stone and she was the eternal, waiting earth.

Acknowledgments

For publishing or commissioning early versions of various pieces included here, I'd like to thank Joanna Yas at *Washington Square Review*, Bradford Morrow at *Conjunctions*, Emily Gould and Ruth Curry at Emily Books, Albert Mobilio and Apex Art, Paula Bomer at *Sententia*, Kelly Jean Fitzsimmons at No, You Tell It!, and the publishers of *Guilt & Pleasure*, who so cleverly introduced me to my phenomenal editor, Nell Casey—back in the days when this book wasn't even yet a viable idea.

For their support and enthusiasm, I would like to thank the community of the MFA program at Fairleigh Dickinson University, where I read out loud most of this material for the first time. In particular I'd like to thank my colleagues and friends René Steinke and Harvey Hix for fierce and dedicated encouragement. My agent, Rebecca Carter, is a beacon and I am grateful to have her by my side. My friends and family have been patient and unwavering—the lot of them far-flung, overseas, and on other coasts, immediate and extended in scores of different, vital ways. I am so grateful for their endurance in my life.